name: _____

Story Map

Characters

Setting

A Letter to Amy
by
Ezra Jack Keats

Problem

Solution

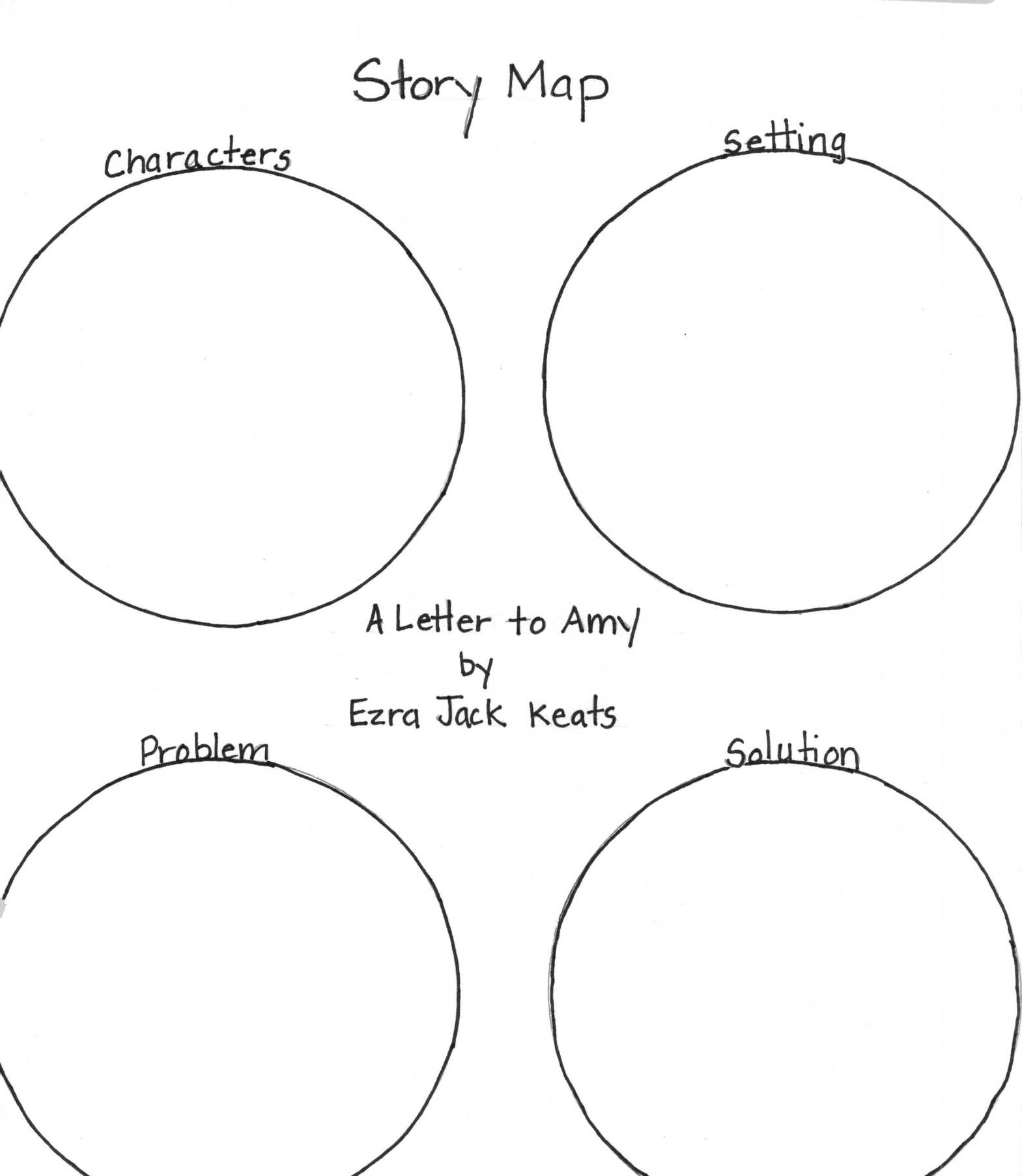

Name: ______________

Story Map

Characters

Setting

A Letter to Amy
by
Ezra Jack Keats

Problem

Solution

Across the Curriculum

with
Favorite Authors

Ezra Jack Keats

Written by Patricia Pecuch

Illustrated by

Agi Palinay

Teacher Created Materials, Inc.
P.O. Box 1040
Huntington Beach, CA   92647
©1995 Teacher Created Materials, Inc.
Made in U.S.A.
ISBN-1-55734-459-0

Table Of Contents

Introduction

Our teaching is enriched daily by the wealth of outstanding authors who give us words and pictures to engage, motivate, and inspire our students. Through these authors, our students become acquainted with worlds and ideas beyond their own and emerge as more aware, active, and enthusiastic readers.

In this author series, one author is spotlighted in each resource book. Teachers and students have the opportunity to participate in an in-depth study of each author's work and style.

Integrated activities across the curriculum are included to make the unit more meaningful to young children. Elements highlighted in this unit include the following:

❑ Biographical information for a closer look at the author's life, style, motivations, and place in literary history

❑ Extensive suggestions and samples for story mapping

❑ In-depth cross-curricular lessons on individual books, according to this format:

—*Book themes*

—*Book summaries*

—*Before-reading-the-book ideas*

—*While-reading-the-book activities*

—*After-reading-the-book ideas*

❑ A bibliography

❑ An answer key

We are confident the author approach to studying literature will be a satisfying experience for you and your students.

Ezra Jack Keats

Crowning a lifelong interest in art, illustration, and children's books, Ezra Jack Keats received in 1980 the University of Southern Mississippi Silver Medallion, awarded on a yearly basis for outstanding contributions in the field of children's books. It is one of many such distinctions in an extensive list of awards and honors for Keats' works, including the Caldecott Medal in 1963 for *The Snowy Day*. As a popular writer and illustrator, he is perhaps best known for his simple stories that say so much. His text and accompanying illustrations capture life as it really is, allowing readers to identify personal experience within the books' covers.

Ezra Jack Keats *(cont.)*

Ezra Jack Keats was born on March 11, 1916. The youngest of three children born to Benjamin and Augusta Keats, he was raised in a rough neighborhood in Brooklyn, New York. His parents had immigrated to the United States from Poland to avoid the persecution of Jewish people there.

By the age of four, Keats showed a flare for being artistic. He would sit at his enamel kitchen table to draw or sketch. Once he painted right across the top of the table—profiles of men, women, children, little houses with curly smoke coming from the chimney—all the things that children usually draw. Soon the whole table top was full! Instead of scolding him when she came into the room, his mother was very interested and pleased with his drawings. She covered the table with a cloth, and when friends or neighbors came to visit, she would uncover it to show off her son's artwork. She continued to encourage him to pursue his artistic talents.

At first, Keats' father disapproved of his wanting to be an artist. Later, however, his father did try to help his son by taking him to art museums and exhibits of work by famous artists and painters. These exhibits did not appeal to Keats, however, for he wanted to capture real things as he saw them and felt about them.

Although Keats had had no formal art training throughout school, he was offered three art scholarships. One of his teachers gave him his first art sketch box, which Keats treasured as a special gift. Even though he was offered the scholarships, he chose to go to work instead.

During the 1930s, he worked as a mural painter on WPA (Works Progress Administration) projects. In the U.S. Air Corps during World War II, he worked as a camouflage expert.

After the war, his first art assignment was a full-color editorial illustration in *Collier's* magazine. He traveled to Europe in 1948, painting extensively. Upon returning to the United States, he exhibited some of his works in the Associated American Artists Galleries in New York. Keats drew for *Captain Marvel* comic books, and he illustrated manuals for the U.S. Army. He then began illustrating books for others. Though he enjoyed this, he often wondered about the complicated, wordy texts. Keats also noticed that many of the authors did not depict realistic characters, few of them having differently colored skins or lifestyles.

Years before he ever considered doing illustrations, Keats had discovered four magazine photographs of a small boy about four years old. He liked these pictures so much that he cut them out and kept them on his studio wall. When he decided to write his own books, these pictures became the basis for his character, Peter, who appears first in *The Snowy Day,* and then in *Peter's Chair, Goggles!,* and *Hi, Cat!* Many of Keats' books have since been made into films, filmstrips, and tapes.

After his death in 1983, the Ezra Jack Keats Foundation established an international award in his name to honor promising future illustrators.

About Story Mapping

Story mapping is another term for identifying the four parts of a fictional story—characters, setting, problem, and solution. These parts are often referred to by various names, such as story elements. Younger children, especially, do not necessarily need to know the exact terms for these parts, but they can easily learn to respond to simple questions about a story instead. Regardless of the age of your students, however, story mapping exercises can help them become better readers by bringing more meaning to the stories they read. Students who use story mapping as a skill can read more critically and understand what they have read. Developing such skills also helps students become better writers themselves. By teaching your students to map out a story, you allow them to make their own choices and decisions about the selections they read. You also have an excellent alternative assessment strategy at your fingertips when you make use of story mapping in the classroom.

The four parts of any fictional story are its characters, setting, problem, and the solution. *Characters* are simply who or what the story is about. They can be people or animals—usually one or two main characters as well as other supporting characters in the story. The *setting* describes where and when the story takes place. The *problem* is the difficulty, crisis, or main event that the character encounters. The *solution* or ending of a story is the part that tells how the problem is (or is not) solved and what happens to the character(s) because of it. Most often we discover information about the characters and setting in the very first pages of the story. The main part of the story revolves around the problem and all the things that take place because of the problem. The solution usually comes at the very end of the story.

A *theme* is the message, lesson, or issue that the author addresses through his story. Not every story will necessarily be written around a theme. All stories (with the exception of those in very early readers that use a controlled vocabulary) will contain the four main story parts.

Teaching Your Students About Story Mapping

To help your students begin to understand and use the skill of story mapping, you may want to use some well-known stories. Classic fairy tales work very well for this. Introduce the names of the four story parts and create a large story map blank or chart on the blackboard or on chart paper.

Story Map Chart	
Characters	
Setting	
Problem	
Solution	

About Story Mapping *(cont.)*

Read a familiar tale such as *Cinderella, Little Red Riding Hood,* or *The Three Little Pigs.* You may wish to use a particular selection that your class has been reading, as well. After rereading the story together and some general discussion, ask key questions to determine each story part. This activity should be done as a total group activity.

Let us use the tale of *The Three Little Pigs* as an example. After reading this together, ask students the following:

- Who is the story about?
- What animals do we hear about in the story?

Record the responses after "Characters" on your chart and explain to students that the three pigs and the wolf are the characters in the story, or who the story is about.

Story Map Chart	
Characters	three pigs, the wolf
Setting	
Problem	
Solution	

Now ask students to describe the setting by asking the following:

- Where does the story take place?
- When does it happen?

Depending on the version of the book you have read, answers such as "in the woods," "a long, long time ago," "by the pigs' houses," "daytime," etc., will most likely be responses to record for the setting. Reinforce to students that the setting always tells where and when the story takes place.

Story Map Chart	
Characters	three pigs, the wolf
Setting	in the woods, daytime
Problem	
Solution	

About Story Mapping *(cont.)*

To help students understand the *problem* of a story, ask them questions such as the following:

- What happened in the story?
- What did the pigs have to worry about?
- What did the pigs do that put them in a dangerous situation?
- What trouble or problem did the pigs face?

Under the problem space on your story map, help students work through the problem in a logical way. (Very rarely is it necessary to use complete sentences when story mapping.)

Story Map Chart	
Characters	three pigs, the wolf
Setting	in the woods, daytime
Problem	The wolf kept blowing the pigs' houses down and trying to eat the pigs!
Solution	

The solution always refers directly to the problem that is described. In some stories there are several smaller sub-problems and solutions within the story. Help your students concentrate on the general or main problem and solution of the story.

After they have determined the problem, prompt your students to tell you the solution by rephrasing the problem in this way:

- Did the pigs' houses get blown down and were they eaten?

Or simply ask these questions:

- What happened in the end?
- How did the story turn out?

Under solution, record the information:

Story Map Chart	
Characters	three pigs, the wolf
Setting	in the woods, daytime
Problem	The wolf kept blowing the pigs' houses down and trying to eat the pigs!
Solution	The pigs hid safely in the last brother's brick house, and they tricked the wolf and killed him.

About Story Mapping *(cont.)*

Review the story map information, and students will begin to see that this is a concise way to retell or recall the story.

You may find it helpful to repeat this step several times over the course of several days or weeks with various stories. Soon students will seem comfortable in determining the four story parts together without as much assistance. At this point you may wish to have students work in small groups with various stories to create small-group story maps. When students are able to complete most story mapping exercises, then they are ready to complete individual story maps on an independent basis as a reading response or as a comprehension check.

Another helpful exercise to do after students have gotten the hang of story mapping is to provide label cards marked CHARACTER, SETTING, PROBLEM, SOLUTION, as well as cards that describe the parts of a particular story or fairy tale they would be familiar with. What students need to do is to simply arrange the cards in the correct spaces next to the corresponding labels. This is an excellent activity to make up and have students do independently as a worksheet or a learning center activity.

As a continued follow-up exercise to story mapping, you can give your students a mixed-up story map, where the story parts are in the wrong places. Their task is to cut and paste (or otherwise arrange) the correct story parts under the correct headings.

As students begin to complete more individual, independent story mapping exercises, always make sure that the four labels—character, setting, problem, solution—are posted somewhere in the room so that they may copy and spell them correctly when needed.

You can always ask students to tell you the four story parts after they have completed reading a story. This is an excellent way to check for comprehension and get a feel for the student's ability to include details and use vocabulary.

As time goes on, it is a very interesting activity to start to compare various stories and authors by looking critically at their story parts. Many authors use the same characters in all their books. Many stories have the same problem or theme but are different otherwise. This is an excellent way to start a discussion or skill work on an author's purpose and style in writing.

Story Mapping and This Book

For each Ezra Jack Keats unit included in this book, a story map is already provided. The answers suggested are possible information to include, but a student's own wording is always encouraged.

Themes and subjects are also listed for each of Keats' books, as well as several blanks for story mapping exercises or practice you may wish to use with your students.

Story Mapping Samples

- Fold a large strip of light colored construction paper into five sections.

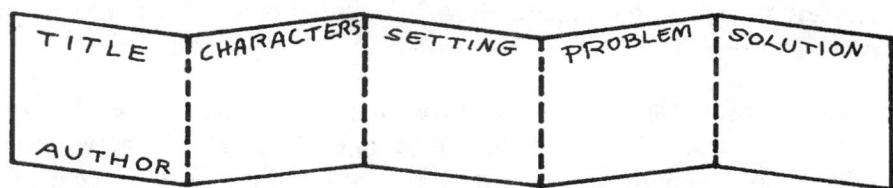

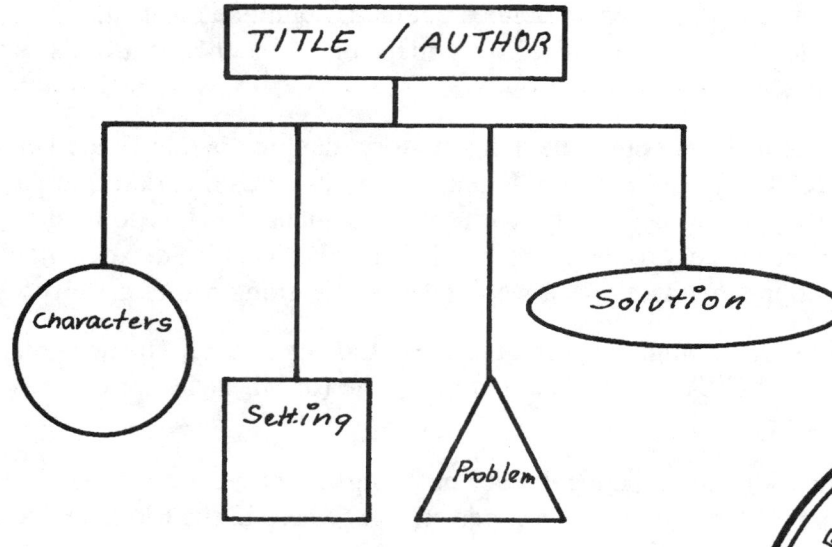

- Make a mobile to hang.

- Encourage students to write on one side and draw a picture of the story event on the other side.

- Section off a paper plate to record the four story elements.

Title Author	Characters	Setting	Problem	Solution

- Make a giant wall poster for a bulletin board or draw a large story map grid on chalkboard.

- Use the grid to compare different stories by Ezra Jack Keats or other authors.

Story Mapping Samples *(cont.)*

Name_____   Date _____

Title _____

Author _____

Characters	Setting
Problem	**Solution**

Story Mapping Samples *(cont.)*

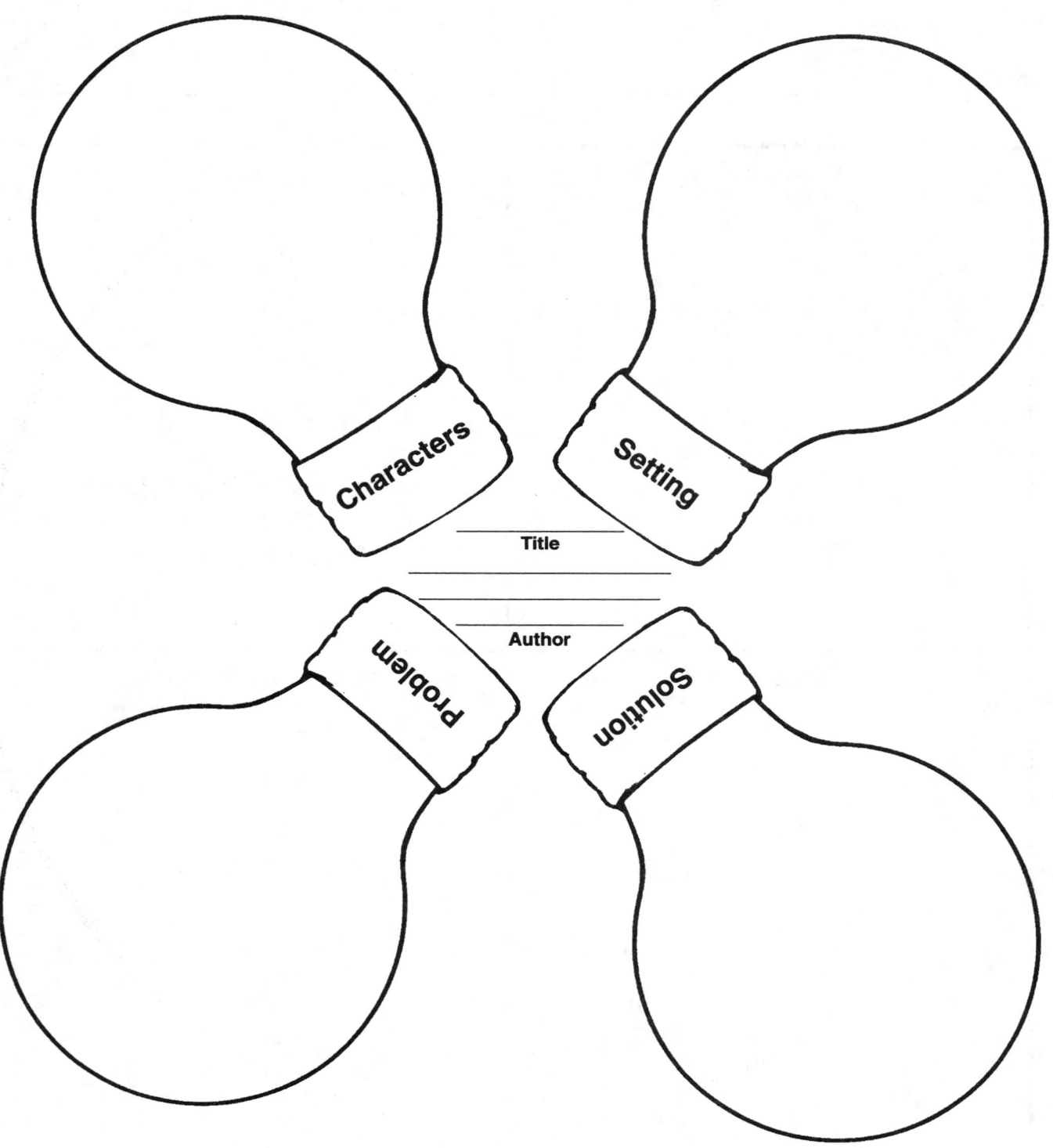

Characters

Setting

Title
_____
_____

Author

Problem

Solution

Story Mapping Samples *(cont.)*

Directions: After reading a story, students enter information (title, author, date, student name) on wheel one. On wheel two, students write or draw information about the four story elements.

Cut out both wheels and attach wheel one on top with a short brass fastener. Turn the wheel to view story map parts.

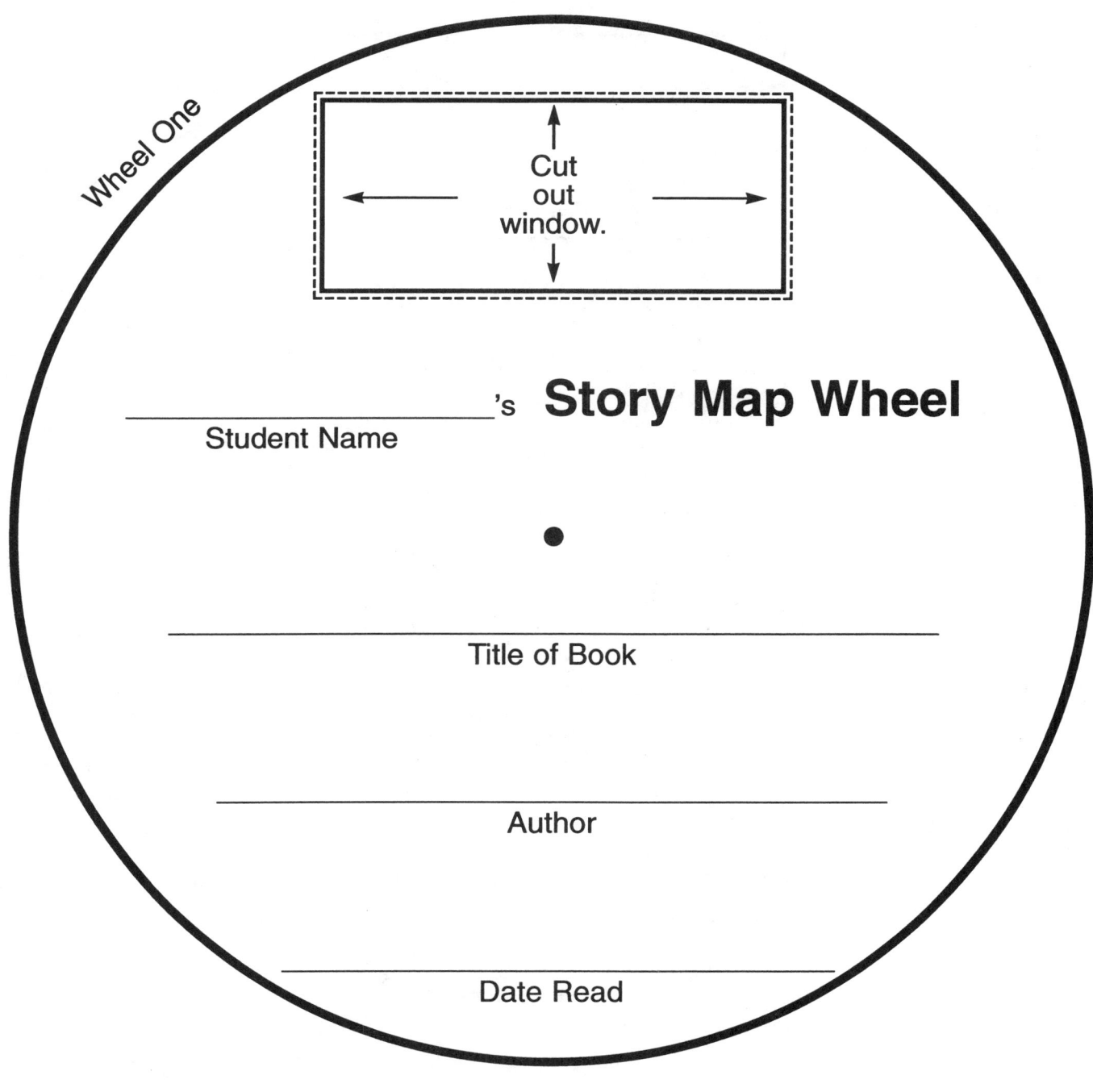

Story Mapping Samples *(cont.)*

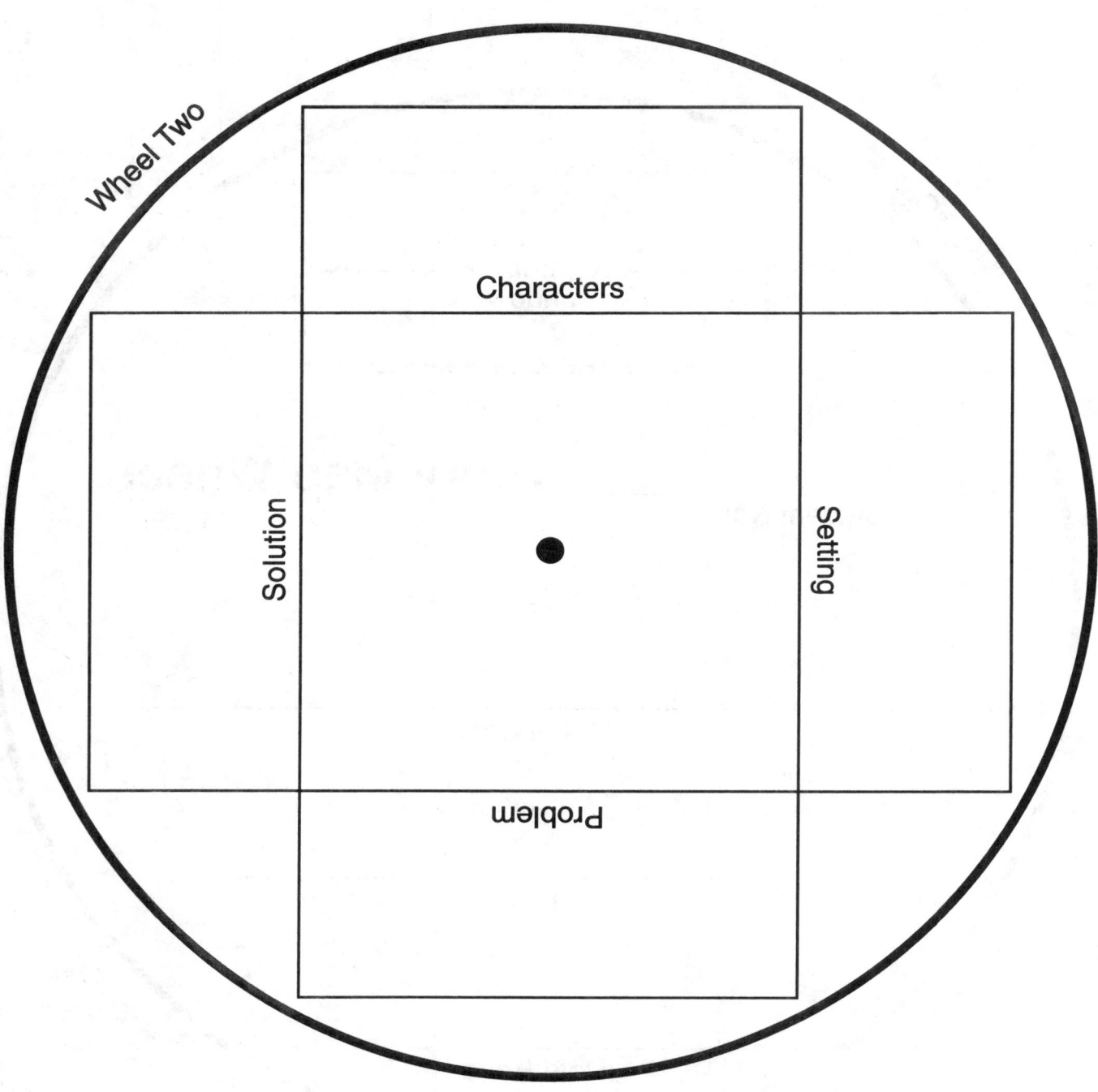

Whistle for Willie

Themes

- Learning Something New
- Patience
- Practicing for Achievements and Talents
- Growing Up

Summary

Peter wants to be able to whistle. He sees another boy who is able to whistle for his dog. Peter wishes that he were able to whistle for his dog, Willie. He tries and tries to whistle but still cannot. Even though he wants to whistle so badly but cannot, Peter keeps practicing and trying. He never gives up. He finds other things to keep himself busy while he continues to attempt to whistle. Finally and unexpectedly, a real whistle comes out, and Peter is able to whistle for his dog to come to him! Peter's parents are proud of his whistling, and Peter continues to enjoy his new-found ability.

Story Map

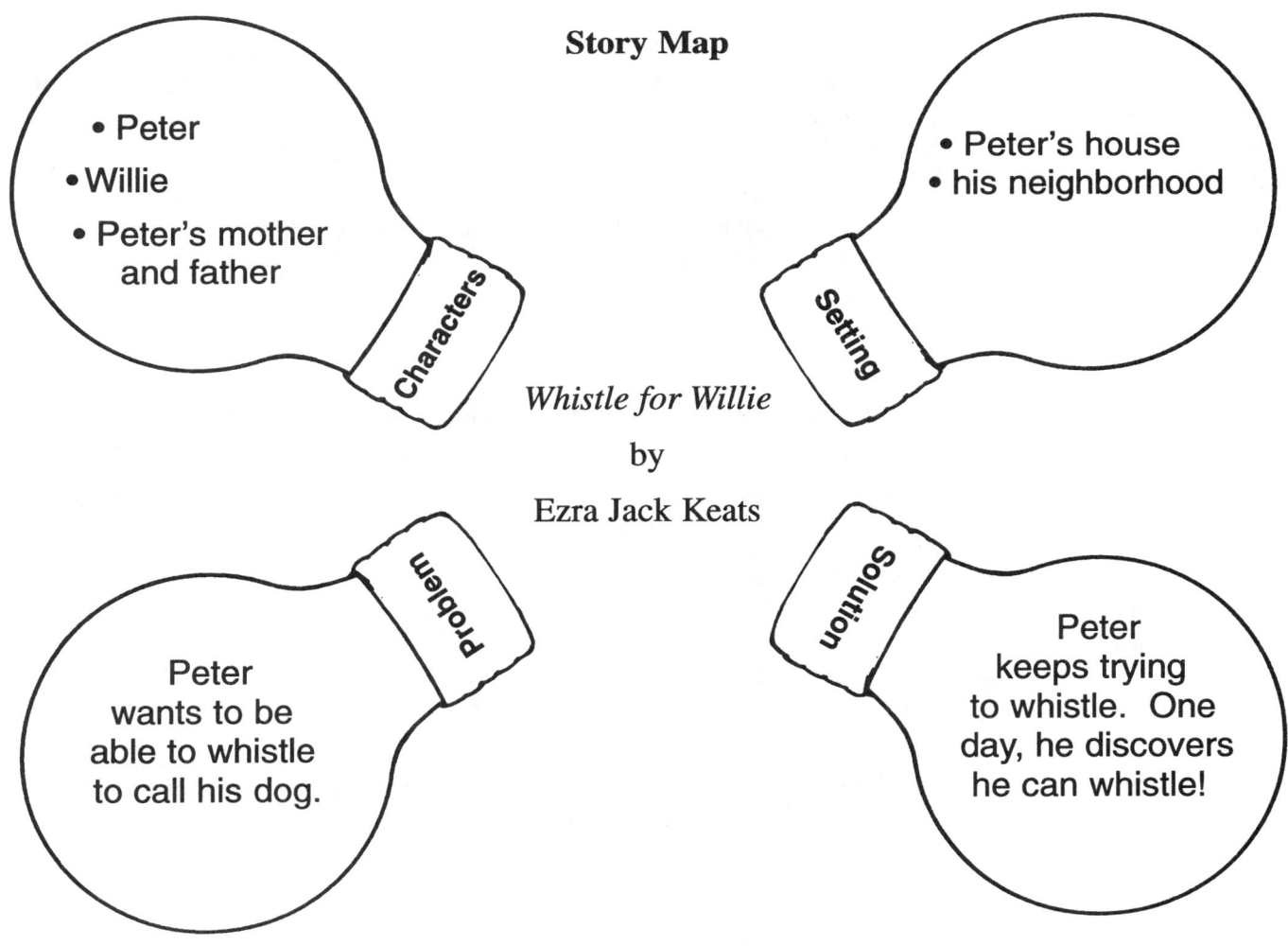

Characters
- Peter
- Willie
- Peter's mother and father

Setting
- Peter's house
- his neighborhood

Whistle for Willie

by

Ezra Jack Keats

Problem

Peter wants to be able to whistle to call his dog.

Solution

Peter keeps trying to whistle. One day, he discovers he can whistle!

Whistle for Willie *(cont.)*

Before Reading the Book

Suggested introductory scripts and activities follow:

- In the story, Peter wants to be able to whistle. How many of you can already whistle? Let's whistle a tune together.

- For those of you who can whistle, do you remember when you could not? How did you feel about not being able to do something you wanted to do or that others could do?

- Whistling, like some other things, can be very hard to learn to do. It takes a lot of patience, practice, and mostly just time.

- Think of something you really wanted or would like to learn to do. Maybe it was something like learning to wink one eye at a time, riding a two-wheel bike, skipping, or playing the piano or a sport. Tell about that time. (See page 19 for related writing activity.)

- Discuss with your students why people whistle. Make a list on the board. (to call a pet or friend, to be happy, to pretend not to be afraid, to show surprise, etc.)

- Name some people who whistle or places where whistles are used: policemen, referees, fire whistles, work whistles, musicians, schools, etc. Discuss with students that at some times and places a whistle can be inappropriate.

- When do you whistle? (or wish you could be able to?)

- Pretend you can whistle a very special sounding whistle to call a special or unusual pet or animal. What kind of animal or creature would answer to your whistle? (See page 21 for related activity.)

Some New and Interesting Words from the Story

whistle	tried	corner
carton	again	happened
walked	blew	errand
wished	empty	shadow
straight	pocket	himself
stopped	raced	hid

Whistle for Willie *(cont.)*

After Reading the Book

Suggested discussion topics and activities follow:

- How does Peter feel at the beginning of the story? How does he feel by the end of the story? Why do his feelings change?

- When Peter tries so hard to whistle but cannot, he feels sad and discouraged. Write a letter to Peter to help him feel better about not being able to whistle.

- Act out a scene from the story when Peter hides under the carton. Willie comes along, but since Peter can't whistle, Willie just walks on by.

- Now act out the scene again when Peter can whistle, and Willie is surprised and runs to Peter. (Suggestion: get a giant cardboard box for a prop)

- When you are bored, waiting around for something, or have a problem, what are some of the things you can do to fill up the extra time or take your mind off your problems? Brainstorm with students and make a list of alternative activities for such circumstances, such as playing a game, meeting a friend, watching TV, listening to music, going for a walk, writing a letter, etc. (See page 18 for a related activity.)

- What would you do with a giant cardboard box or carton if you had one? What are some uses for such a box? (See page 21 for a related thinking/writing/drawing activity.)

- What does Peter do to pretend he is his dad?

- Have you ever done anything to feel more grown up than you were? (play with older kids, wear something belonging to an older sibling or parents, etc.)

- What kinds of things can grown-ups do that kids cannot do? Make a list together. These ideas make great raw material to illustrate and put together as a classroom big book. Possible titles might be "Grown-Ups Can, but Kids Can't!" or "I Wish I Were Grown Up So I Could . . . ."

What Would You Do?

We all get angry, confused, or frustrated at times. Think about each situation and pick the best response.

> You are playing ball at school, but you hardly ever get a chance to hit the ball. You . . .
>
> A. start yelling, crying, and screaming at your coach or classmates.
>
> B. cut to the front of the line, grab the ball, and take a turn anyway.
>
> C. remind yourself to be patient and wait for your turn.

> You forgot to study for a test, so when your teacher passes the test out, you…
>
> A. decide to cheat by copying from a friend's paper.
>
> B. do your best on the test anyway and talk to the teacher about it later.
>
> C. pretend you are sick and go to the nurse's office.

Discuss the following situations with your class or group and tell what you would do if you were involved with each problem.

> Just before you get your lunch in the cafeteria, another classmate cuts in line in front of you and takes the last piece of pizza.

> You are helping the teacher by carrying some supplies to the office. On your way, another student runs into you, and you drop some of the supplies. You notice that some of the things are broken.

> Your class is learning a new math skill. Everyone seems to know how to do it except you. You try to understand it, but you cannot.

> You are invited to a friend's house to sleep overnight, but you are afraid to go.

Writing a Paragraph

Answer each question below in a complete sentence. Remember to use capital letters and periods with your sentences.

Think of a time when you learned or wanted to learn how to do something:

Learning to _____

❑ What did you want to learn to do? _____

_____

❑ How old were you then? _____

❑ Why did you want to learn how to do this? _____

_____

❑ Who helped you? _____

_____

❑ Describe the first time you could do it. _____

_____

_____

_____

❑ How did learning this make you feel? _____

_____

Use your answers (in complete sentences) to write a paragraph or story. Use another sheet of writing paper for your paragraph. Draw a picture to go along with your story.

Writing Contractions

Use contractions from the story to fill in each sentence below.

1. Peter _____ whistle.

2. " _____ go play alone," said Peter.

3. " _____ it be funny if I could whistle for Willie?" thought Peter.

4. Mother said, " _____ outside!"

5. " _____ come home from work early today," he said.

6. _____ hard to whistle!

he's	**Wouldn't**	**I'll**
It's	**couldn't**	**I've**

What If . . .

Complete each sentence below and draw a picture to go along with it.

A. If I had a giant cardboard box at
   my house, I would . . .

_____

_____

_____

_____

B. If we had a giant carton or box in
   our classroom, we could . . .

_____

_____

_____

_____

C. If I had a magical whistle, I would
   use it to call . . .

_____

_____

_____

_____

Compound Hounds

Circle the compound word on each dog. See if you can draw a line between the two small words in each compound.

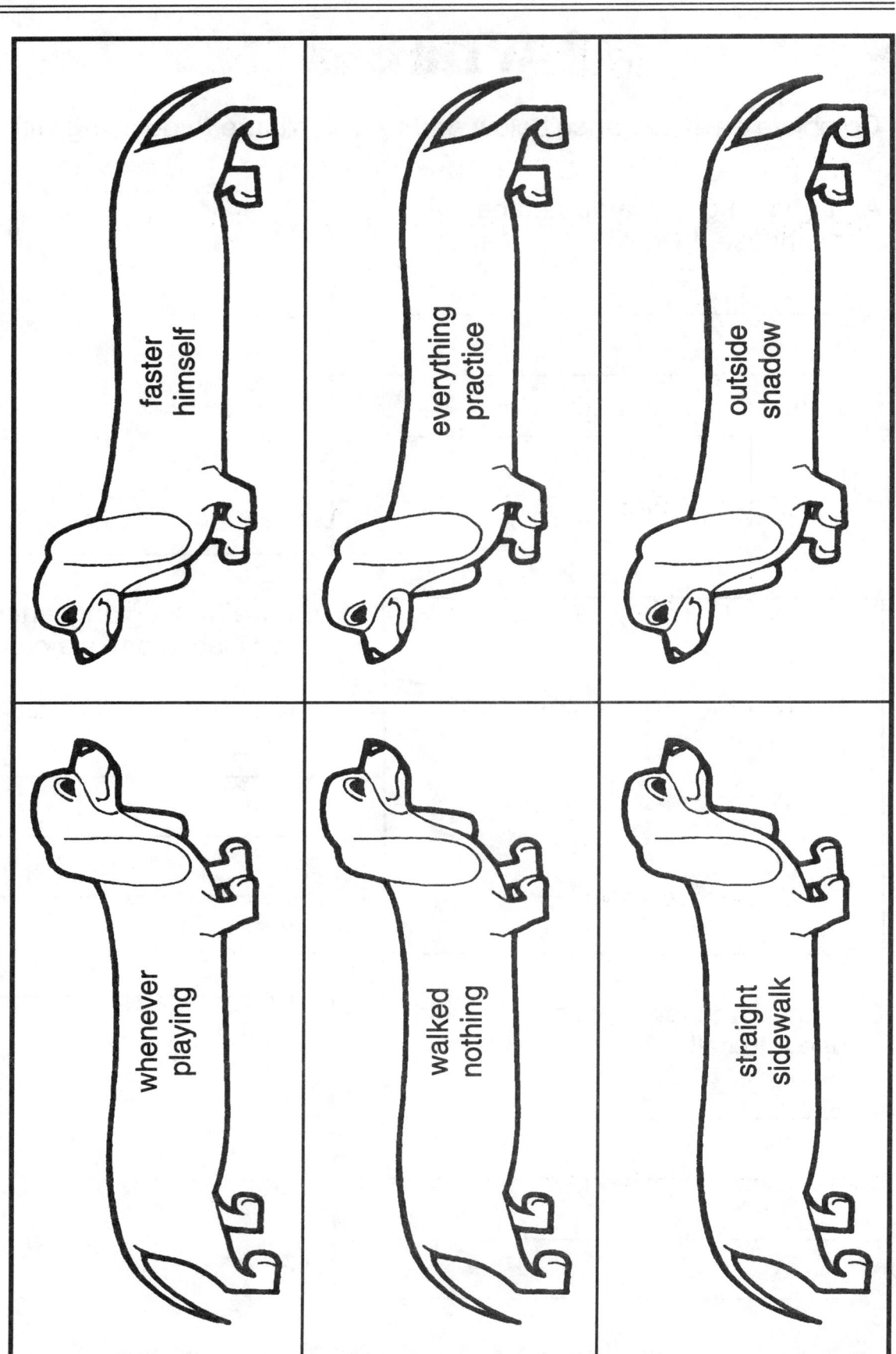

faster
himself

whenever
playing

everything
practice

walked
nothing

outside
shadow

straight
sidewalk

Kids Grow Up . . .

Draw a blue circle around the things that are for kids. Draw a red box around the things that are more for grown-ups. Then discuss them with your friends or class.

(Are there any things in the list that could be for both?)

❏ drive a car ❏ pay bills

❏ play with marbles ❏ have fun

❏ homework ❏ stay up late at night

❏ ride a bike ❏ go to school

❏ wear high-heeled shoes ❏ be president of the United States

❏ have a job ❏ swim

❏ carry a wallet ❏ read

❏ cry ❏ go to college

❏ watch TV

Name some other things for the list:

❏

❏

❏

Real or Make-Believe?

In the story Peter wishes to be able to whistle. This is a wish for something that could really happen, and eventually Peter can whistle! Some wishes are for real things that we really have or will be able to have, and other wishes are just for fun or make-believe.

Color in the space which tells whether the following wishes are real or make-believe.

Wishes	Real	Make-Believe
A wish to fly		
A wish to play baseball better		
A wish for a lot of money		
A wish to take a trip		
A wish for magic powers		
A wish to travel back to the age of dinosaurs		
A wish to live somewhere else		
A wish to be president		
A wish to be Cinderella at the ball		
A wish to be a whale in the ocean		
A wish to ride a boat across an ocean		
A wish to change your height		
A wish to live in a castle		
A wish to become a movie star		
A wish to visit a foreign country		
A wish to read better		

Sequencing

Number the events in each box in the same order that they happen in the story. Look in the book if you need to.

_____ Peter hid in an empty carton but still could not whistle.

_____ Peter saw another boy whistle for his dog.

_____ Peter turned himself around and around and got dizzy.

_____ Peter drew a long, long line with some colored chalk.

_____ Peter tried to run away from his shadow.

_____ Peter put his dad's hat on to feel more grown up.

_____ Willie raced straight to Peter when he heard the whistle.

_____ Peter showed his parents he could whistle.

_____ Peter whistled all the way to the store and back.

_____ Peter hid under the carton again, and a real whistle came out!

Jennie's Hat

Themes

- Gifts
- Disappointment
- Nature
- Animal Friends
- Beauty

Summary

Thinking about the wonderful new hat her aunt has promised to send her as a present, Jennie is excited! When the hat arrives, however, Jennie is greatly disappointed to discover that it is rather plain. She stuffs that hat away and tries on other things that might do for a fancier hat, such as a lampshade and a pot. She sees other ladies with beautiful hats all around her.

Forgetting her hat problems, Jennie remembers that it is time to go to the park to feed her friends, the birds, as she does each Saturday afternoon. The next day she wears her plain hat to church. As she leaves the church, the birds flutter around her and decorate her hat with flowers, pictures, leaves, eggs, and colored paper. Jennie's hat turns out to be beautiful and fancy after all!

Story Map

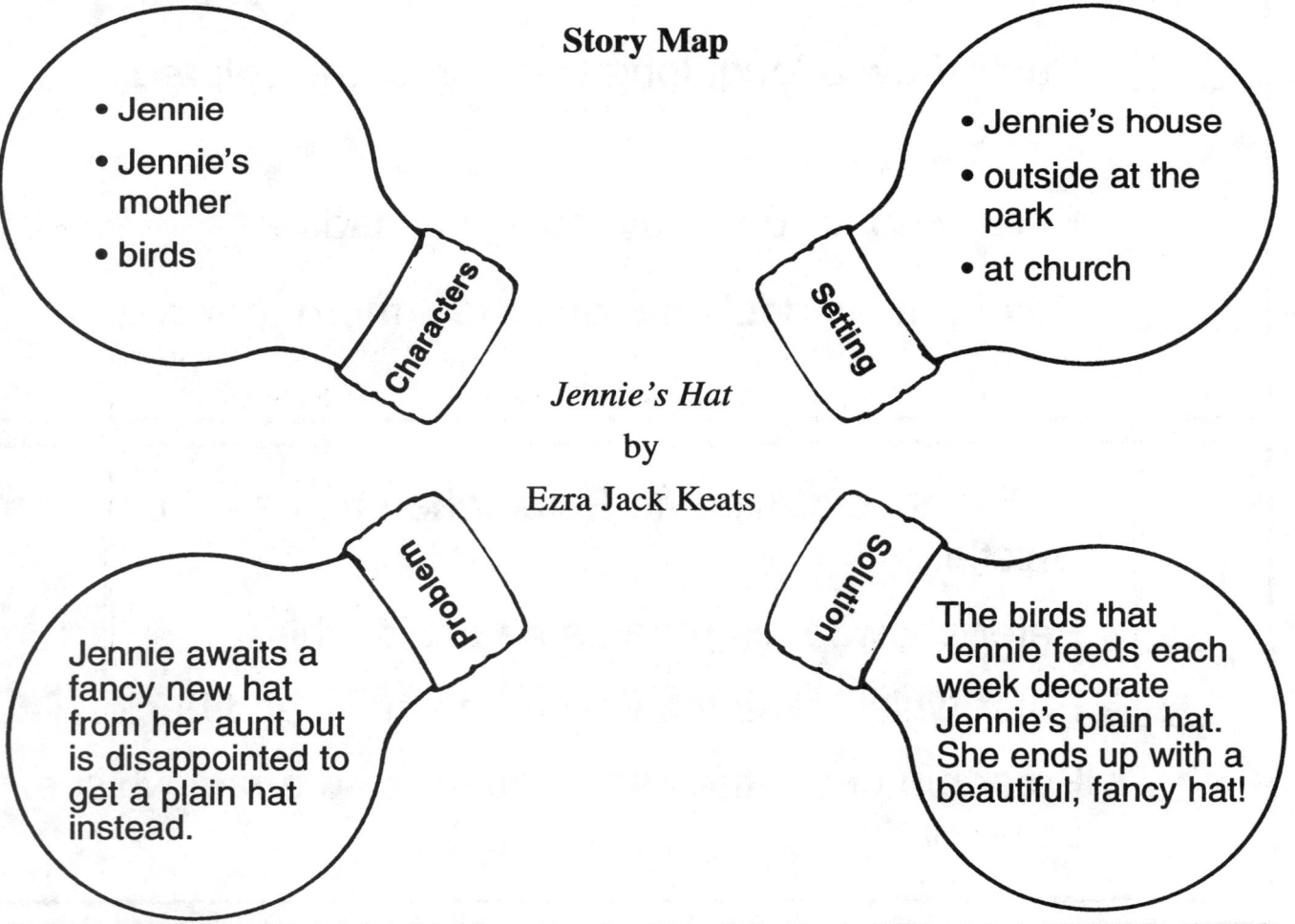

Characters
- Jennie
- Jennie's mother
- birds

Setting
- Jennie's house
- outside at the park
- at church

Jennie's Hat
by
Ezra Jack Keats

Problem
Jennie awaits a fancy new hat from her aunt but is disappointed to get a plain hat instead.

Solution
The birds that Jennie feeds each week decorate Jennie's plain hat. She ends up with a beautiful, fancy hat!

Jennie's Hat *(cont.)*

Before Reading the Book

Suggested introductory scripts and activities follow:

- How might you feel if you were expecting a special present from someone?

- Pretend someone is going to buy you a new hat. Draw a picture of how you would like your new hat to look.
  (For increased motivation, bring in a special or unique looking hat in a hat box or brown paper bag. Discuss what it might look like, but delay revealing it until the drawings are completed.)

- Have any of you ever pictured something one way, and then (when you actually saw it) found that it looked different from what you had expected? Sometimes we get so excited about getting gifts or about an event that we picture them differently in our heads than they really are.

- In the story, a little girl named Jennie feeds the birds at the park every week. How many of you have a birdfeeder or feed the birds at your house? In what other ways can we help the animals?

- Make a mini-birdfeeder to hang at home. (See page 33.)

- Let's list as many different kinds of birds as we can.

- Should we always feel grateful when we receive gifts?

- How should we show our thanks for receiving gifts?

- How does giving gifts make us feel?

- Suppose we gave someone a gift and that person did not seem happy or pleased. How would we feel?

Some New and Interesting Words from the Story

favorite	plain	lovely
aunt	fancier	added
present	straw	paper
dreamed	expected	real
waited	wished	colored
beautiful		

Jennie's Hat *(cont.)*

After Reading the Book

Suggested discussion topics and activities follow:

- Make (decorate) a large paper hat for a bulletin board, wall, or door hanging.

- Ask students to design and create their own hats at home from miscellaneous materials and have an unusual hat show or parade. (You can tie in this idea with spring or a holiday parade. It is also fun to have students create their own original hats in class from recyclable items brought from home—buttons, pieces of felt, lace, ribbons, sequins, yarn, fabric flowers, leather, plastic, etc.)

- What does Jennie wish for? What kind of hat does her aunt send her? How does Jennie feel about the hat? Should she be angry with her aunt?

- In the story, the birds help Jennie decorate her plain hat. Why do you think the birds do that?

- Can any of you think of a time when an animal helped you or someone else? (Describe accounts of dogs fetching things or being heroes, cats bringing mice or other things as "gifts" for their owners, horses pulling wagons, etc. Perhaps you can add examples from television shows or movies.)

- When Jennie discovers her hat is a plain one instead of the fancy one she has imagined it to be, she feels disappointed and blinks back tears.

- How many other ways do we show that we are disappointed or sad? (tears, voice, actions, etc.)

- Have students role play Jennie getting the hat in person from her aunt. You may wish to role play or discuss other emotions—happiness, fear, worry, love—and how we show our feelings in various situations.

Sequencing

After reading the story, cut apart the eight cards. Arrange them in the same order as the events happened in the story.

Jennie tries on other things to use for a hat.	Jennie waits for her hat to come.
She opens the box she got from her aunt.	Jennie goes to church with her family.
The birds decorate Jennie's hat for her.	Jennie and her mother wrap her wonderful hat.
Jennie feeds the birds on Saturday afternoon.	Jennie thinks her hat is too plain.

Opposites

For each of the words below, choose an opposite word from the hatbox below.
Write that opposite word on the correct line.

fancy	_____	aunt	_____
beautiful	_____	add	_____
appeared	_____	real	_____
shutting	_____	big	_____
opened	_____	mother	_____
shiny	_____	started	_____
same	_____	filled	_____
early	_____	quiet	_____
proud	_____	after	_____

- before
- emptied
- dull
- little
- father
- uncle
- ashamed
- fake
- plain
- ugly
- late
- loud
- disappeared
- different
- opening
- subtract
- closed
- ostopped

Is That on Her Hat?

Can you remember all the things Jennie had on her hat when the birds decorated it for her? If the space tells something Jennie had on her hat, color it orange. If it is not something on her hat, color it blue.

leaves	a big orange leaf	brown weeds	a coin	a twig
a stone	violet flowers	a piece of newspaper	three buttons	striped ribbon
a paper fan	a big red rose	a frog	a flashlight	a bag of crumbs
a pink Valentine	some dirt	more real flowers	picture of swans on a lake	paper flowers
a big green leaf	a nest of chirping birds	colored eggs	a blue butterfly	a big yellow rose
tree bark	a caterpillar	a flower pot	birdseed	more pictures
a straw basket	a paper bag	a staple	a paper clip	colored paper

Jennie's Family

Match pairs of relatives' names on each pair of hats. The name of the female relative should be written on the bonnet. The male relative's name is to be written on the derby.

mother	aunt	daughter	nephew
grandfather	niece	father	brother
sister	son	grandmother	uncle

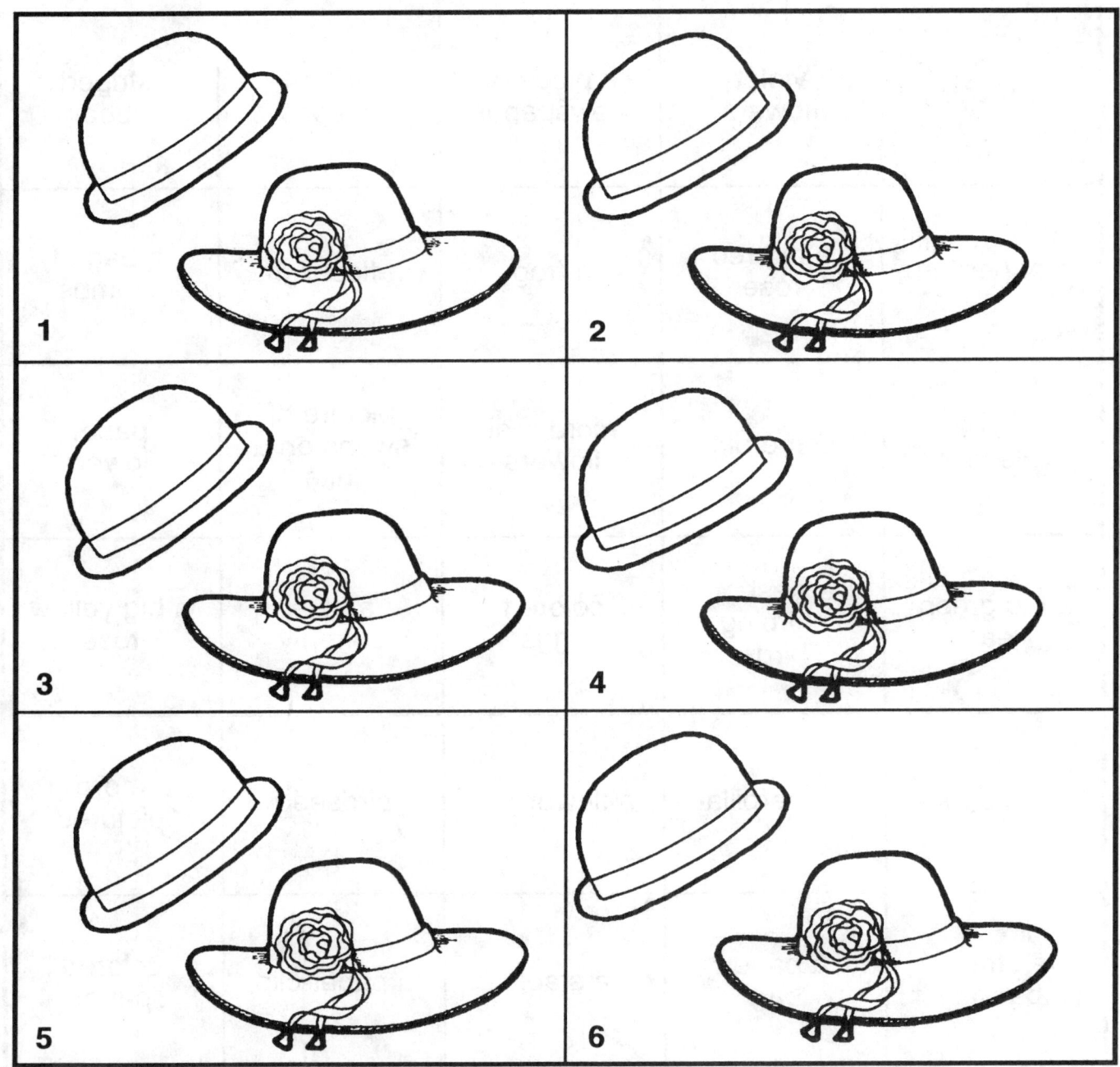

Make a Pinecone Bird Feeder

In the story, Jennie feeds the birds each Saturday afternoon.

You can be kind to the birds around your own house or neighborhood by hanging up a birdfeeder.

Materials Needed:

- a pinecone (A dried one with open spaces between each layer works best.)
- string
- peanut butter
- birdseed

Directions:

1. Tie a string to the smaller, top end of the pinecone.

2. Using a plastic knife or butter knife, spread peanut butter over the cone and between each layer.

3. Roll the pinecone in a shallow dish filled with birdseed.

4. Hang it from a tree branch or bush and watch the birds gather for a special treat!

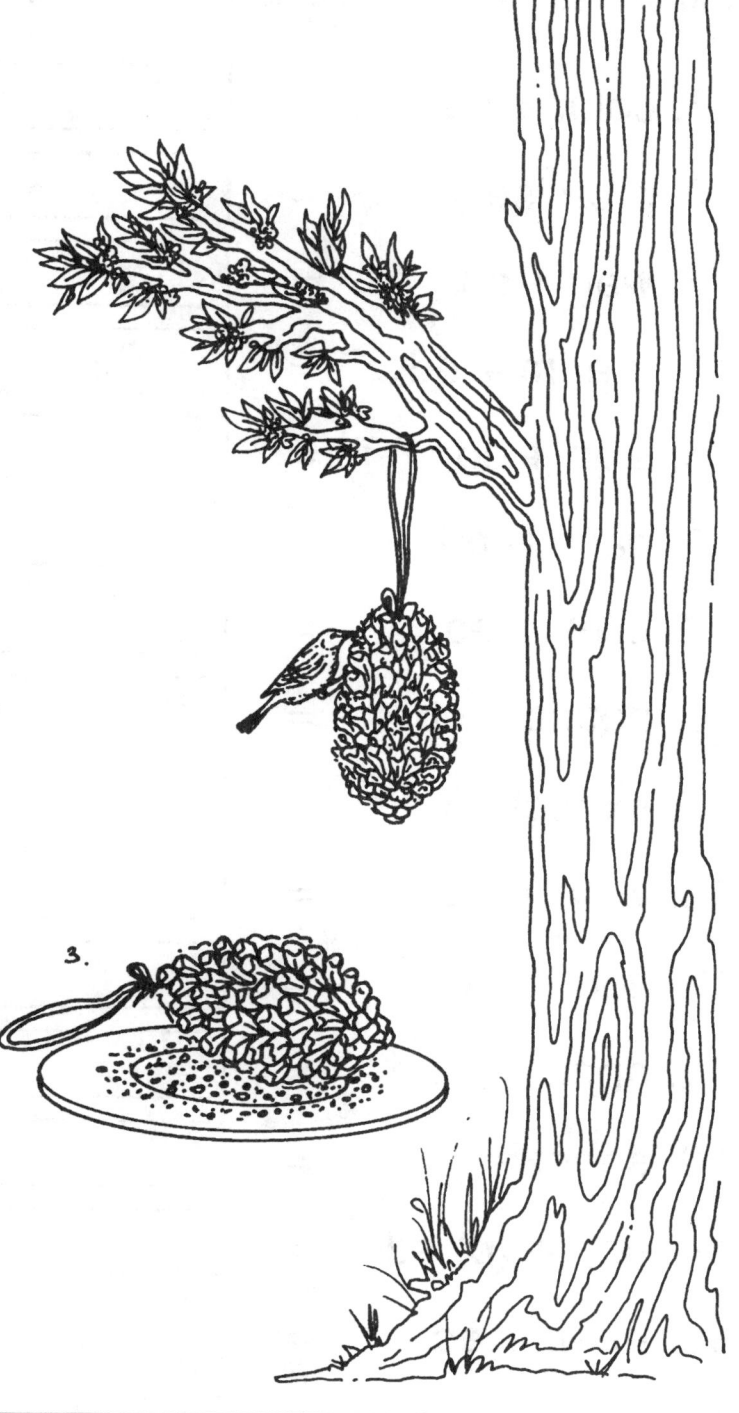

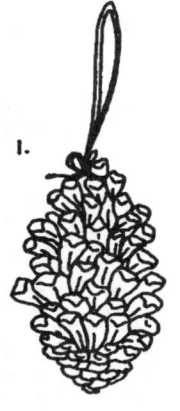

Word Endings

When you add an *-ed* ending to words, sometimes it sounds like a *t*. It can also sound like a *d*. The *-ed* ending can also add another syllable when you pronounce the vowel and make the ending sound like the name "Ed."

Add an *-ed* ending to each word and write the new word. Then circle the sound you hear at the end of the new word you wrote.

1. color + ed   =   [   ]   t   d   ed

2. promise + ed   =   [   ]   t   d   ed

3. wait + ed   =   [   ]   t   d   ed

4. dream + ed   =   [   ]   t   d   ed

5. sigh + ed   =   [   ]   t   d   ed

6. gasp + ed   =   [   ]   t   d   ed

7. blink + ed   =   [   ]   t   d   ed

8. notice + ed   =   [   ]   t   d   ed

9. expect + ed   =   [   ]   t   d   ed

10. wish + ed   =   [   ]   t   d   ed

11. add + ed   =   [   ]   t   d   ed

12. appear + ed   =   [   ]   t   d   ed

13. sneeze + ed   =   [   ]   t   d   ed

14. hop + (p) ed   =   [   ]   t   d   ed

15. peep + ed   =   [   ]   t   d   ed

Peter's Chair

Summary

Now that there is a new baby sister, Susie, things are different in Peter's family.

Peter does not feel as important or as noticed as he was when he was the only child. Poor Peter has to play more quietly, and to top things off, all his old belongings are being painted pink and given to his baby sister. He grabs his old blue chair and runs away with it before it, too, can be painted and given away to his sister. His mother calls him back home, and Peter then gets to sit in a grown-up chair to enjoy a special lunch with his mom and dad. Peter realizes he has outgrown his chair in more ways than one, so he suggests to his father that together they paint his old (little) chair pink for his sister, Susie.

Story Map

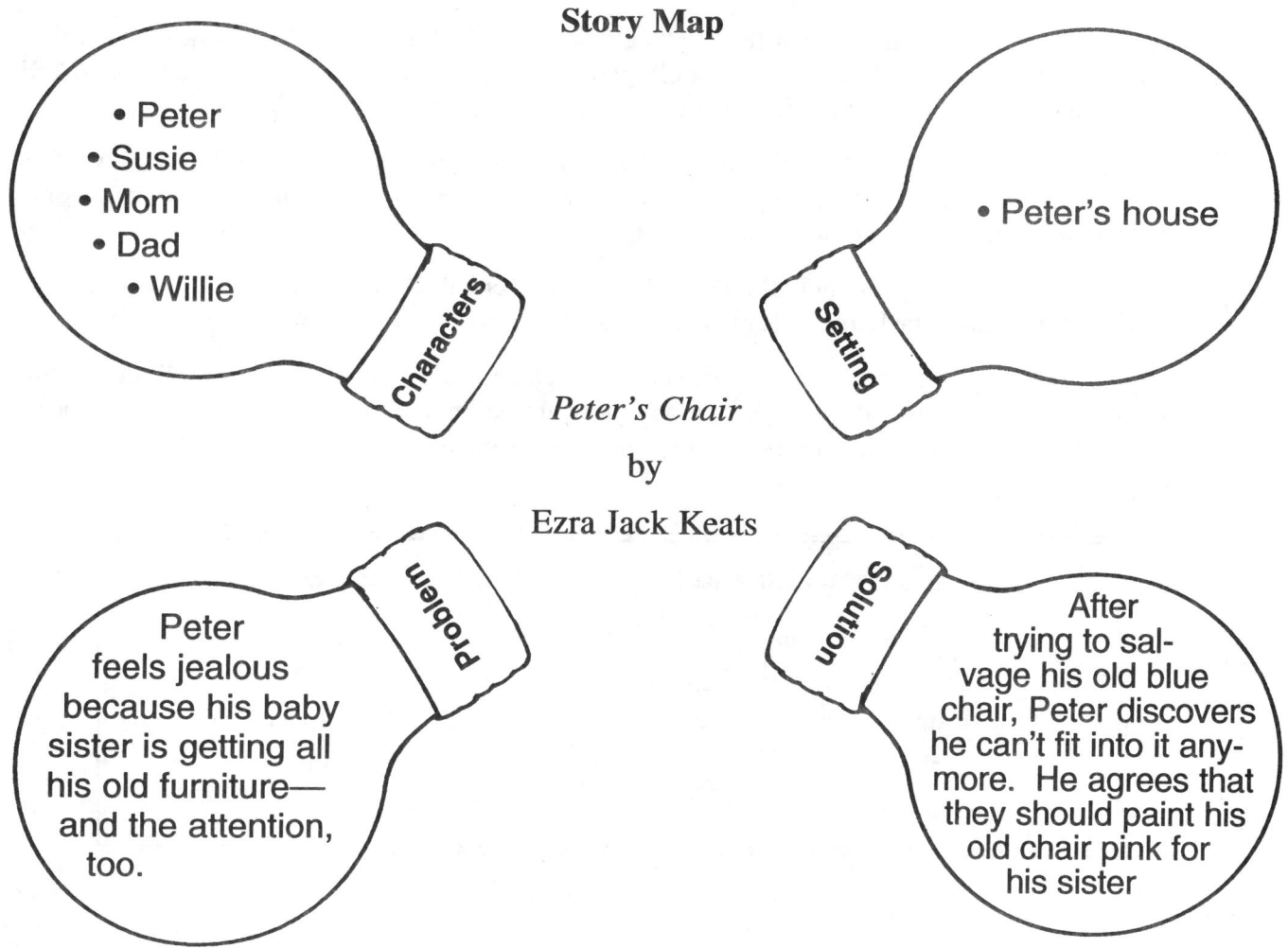

Characters
- Peter
- Susie
- Mom
- Dad
- Willie

Setting
- Peter's house

Peter's Chair

by

Ezra Jack Keats

Problem

Peter feels jealous because his baby sister is getting all his old furniture—and the attention, too.

Solution

After trying to salvage his old blue chair, Peter discovers he can't fit into it anymore. He agrees that they should paint his old chair pink for his sister

Peter's Chair *(cont.)*

Before Reading the Book

Suggested introductory scripts and activities follow:

- Ask students to think about how a new baby in a family could change things. Allow time for students to relate actual experiences.

- Discuss (in general) the composition of families and the concept of what a family really is. Suggest or stress that families are all different and unique, and it is not who makes up the family that is most important but how they feel and act towards one another.

- With the students, create a graph regarding brothers and sisters. (Be sensitive to extended families and count step- and half-siblings). Possible categories to survey and graph could be the numbers of brothers, sisters, only children, those living with one parent, those living with two parents, those living with other adults, and the numbers of older or younger siblings, etc.

- Ask students to give their opinions regarding whether they feel it is better to be older, younger, or in the middle of a family.

- Ask students if they know what feeling "jealous" means. What are the differences between sadness, anger, and jealousy? Why would people feel jealous sometimes? Have students tell or write about a time when they felt jealous.

- Have you ever felt like running away? Why do you think people would want to run away? (Emphasize the reality and safety aspects of running away). What are some of the bad—or even dangerous things—about trying to run away?

- What would you pack up and take with you if you decided to leave home? What would you miss most about your home or family if you left?

- What are some of the students' favorite colors? (Once again, this makes an excellent graphing activity.) Ask students if they think some colors are better suited for kids or for adults, for girls or for boys? Explore the idea of stereotypes with colors, careers, toys, etc.

Some New and Interesting Words from the Story		
building	called	shouted
cradle	quietly	idea
arranged	chair	special
finished	signs	high
painted	sister	pink

Peter's Chair *(cont.)*

After Reading the Book

Suggested discussion topics and activities follow:

- How do you think Peter feels when his mother asks him to play more quietly? Do you think Peter feels jealous? Why? Why do his parents repaint his crib, cradle, and high chair? Would Peter feel differently if they had painted the furniture a color other than pink?

- Why do you think Peter grabs his chair and takes it to his room?

- Why does he decide to run away

- Peter takes some special things with him when he leaves. Can you name them? Tell why you think he takes each one.

- Have students write stories or create a book titled "Why I Like My Home . . . ."

- Do you think Peter loves his baby sister, Susie?

- At the end of the story, Peter suggests to his father that together they go ahead and paint his old blue chair. Why do you think Peter changes his mind about his chair?

- Do you think Peter's parents feel differently about him since his sister was born?

- Peter discovers he has "outgrown" his chair in more ways than one. Besides just being too big to sit in it, what are some other ways Peter feels he has outgrown the chair? What things have you outgrown? What are some things you do differently now that you are older? (See activity sheet Now and Then, page 41.)

- Use the activity sheet Now and Then to create a bulletin board display, make a book to share, or use as a journal entry. Ask students to bring in baby pictures.

- What does Peter learn about being the oldest or growing up in his family? Have students create pages in a class book, telling their position in the family and something positive about the family. When the book is finished, have students take turns taking it home to share with their families.

- Explain what it means to have something "passed down" or a tradition across generations. Ask students to find out if any of them have something special in their family that has been passed down from child to child or among family members. (e.g., rocking horse, crib, cradle, christening gown, jewelry, book, etc.)

Sequencing Practice

Here are eight things that happened in the story. Cut the sentence strips apart and put them in the order that they happened.

Pick one of the events listed on a sentence strip and draw a picture to go with it.

A. Peter notices his old crib and high chair have been painted pink for his sister.

B. Peter and his father paint the blue chair pink.

C. Peter finds out his old blue chair is too small for him to sit in.

D. Peter makes a tall building that crashes to the floor.

E. Peter eats lunch in a grown-up chair next to his father.

F. Peter sees his old blue chair and runs away with it.

G. His mother tells him to play more quietly.

H. Peter's mother calls him back home for lunch.

Who Owns It?

The things below belong to Peter, Susie, or Willie. Next to each item write the name of who owns it now.

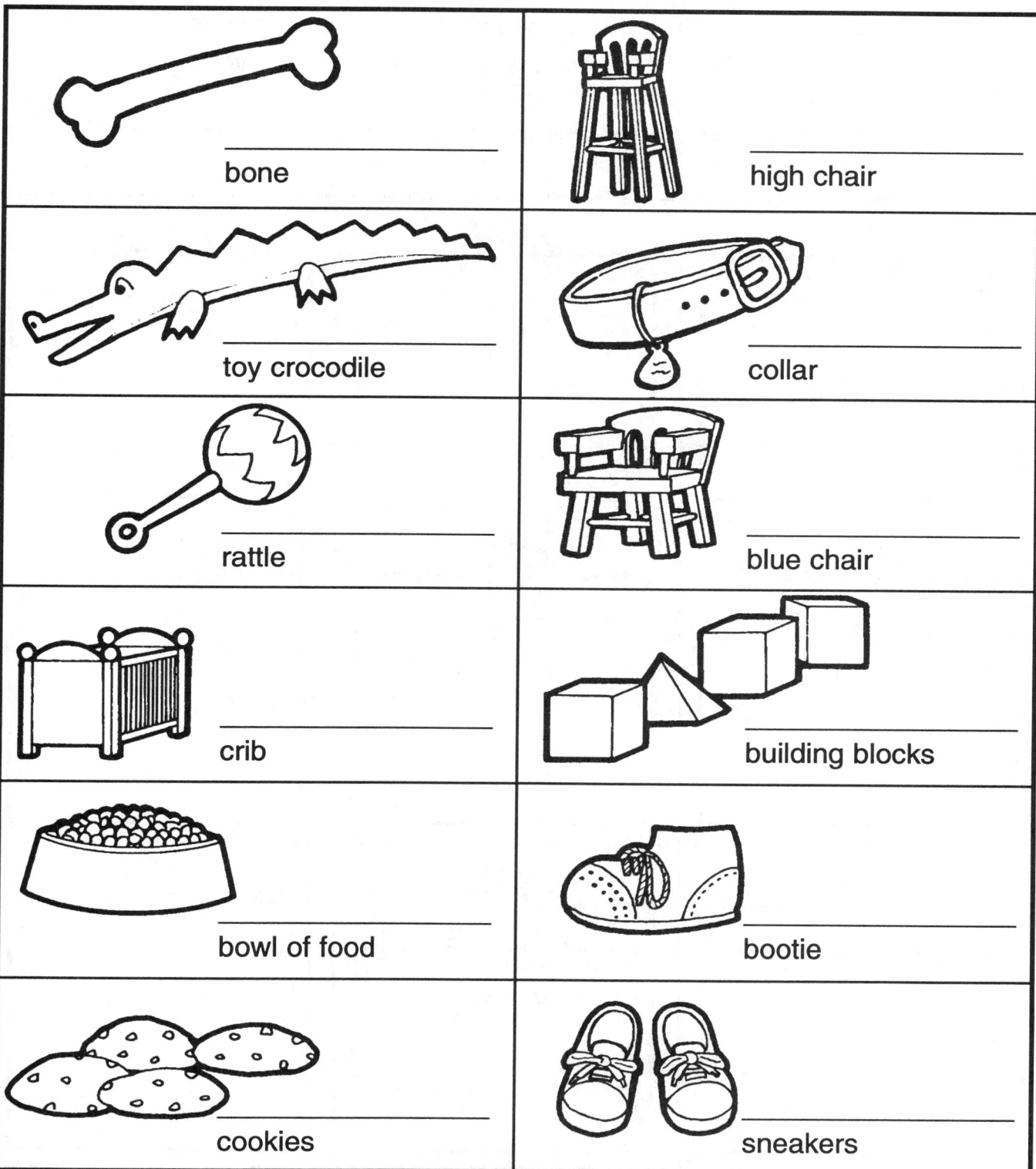

bone

high chair

toy crocodile

collar

rattle

blue chair

crib

building blocks

bowl of food

bootie

cookies

sneakers

Shopping for Contractions

Write the contraction for the two words on each shopping bag.

you'll	wasn't	couldn't
it's	that's	won't
we'll	didn't	

Example:

let us

let's _____

did not

_____

we will

_____

it is

_____

could not

_____

that is

_____

will not

_____

you will

_____

was not

_____

Now and Then

Use words from the box that might tell what you did when you were a baby, compared to what you do now.

baby food	remember	forget	bottle
bicycle	cup	read	crib
bed	pizza	rocking horse	listen

❑ When I was younger, I ate _____,

but now I eat _____.

❑ When I was a baby, I slept in a _____, but

now I sleep in a _____.

❑ I used to drink milk from a _____, but

now I use a _____.

❑ I used to ride on a _____, but

now I ride on my _____.

❑ When I was younger, I used to _____ to my

favorite stories, but now I can _____ some

by myself.

❑ I used to _____ to brush my teeth, but

now I _____ to brush them each day.

❑ **Bonus:** When I was younger, I _____, but

now I _____.

Opposites

Use the cards on this page and the next. Have students cut out each of the cards and turn them all face down. Students can work in pairs or small groups taking turns trying to find two cards that list opposites.

start	high	quietly	baby
sister	leave	tall	do
whispered	stood	full	happy
ceiling	mother	outside	front

Opposites *(cont.)*

Use the cards on this page and the one before this to have students work on matching opposite words. As a variation, teachers may wish to paste words on heavier cards to use as a classroom activity or game in a center.

father	don't	stay	sat
sad	floor	brother	yelled
back	empty	adult	loudly
inside	low	finish	short

A Letter to Amy

Themes

- Friends
- Birthdays
- Having Confidence in Yourself
- Communication
- Parties

Summary

Peter is having a birthday party and writes a special invitation letter to Amy—the only girl he is inviting. He leaves his house to mail the letter, but a rain-and-wind storm comes up and he almost loses the letter. While trying to catch the letter, he runs into Amy and knocks her down on the wet ground. He grabs the letter quickly so she will not see it, and he quickly mails it. When Peter turns around to look for Amy, she has already run off crying. Peter worries that now Amy will not come to his party and even wonders whether he has done the right thing by inviting her. The day of the party comes, and Peter is disappointed that Amy has not arrived. Amy finally comes to Peter's party—a little late—and everyone has a good time together after all. When it comes time for Peter's mother to bring out the cake with candles, his friends suggest things he should wish for. Peter makes his own wish, however, leaving the reader wondering just exactly what he wishes for!

Story Map

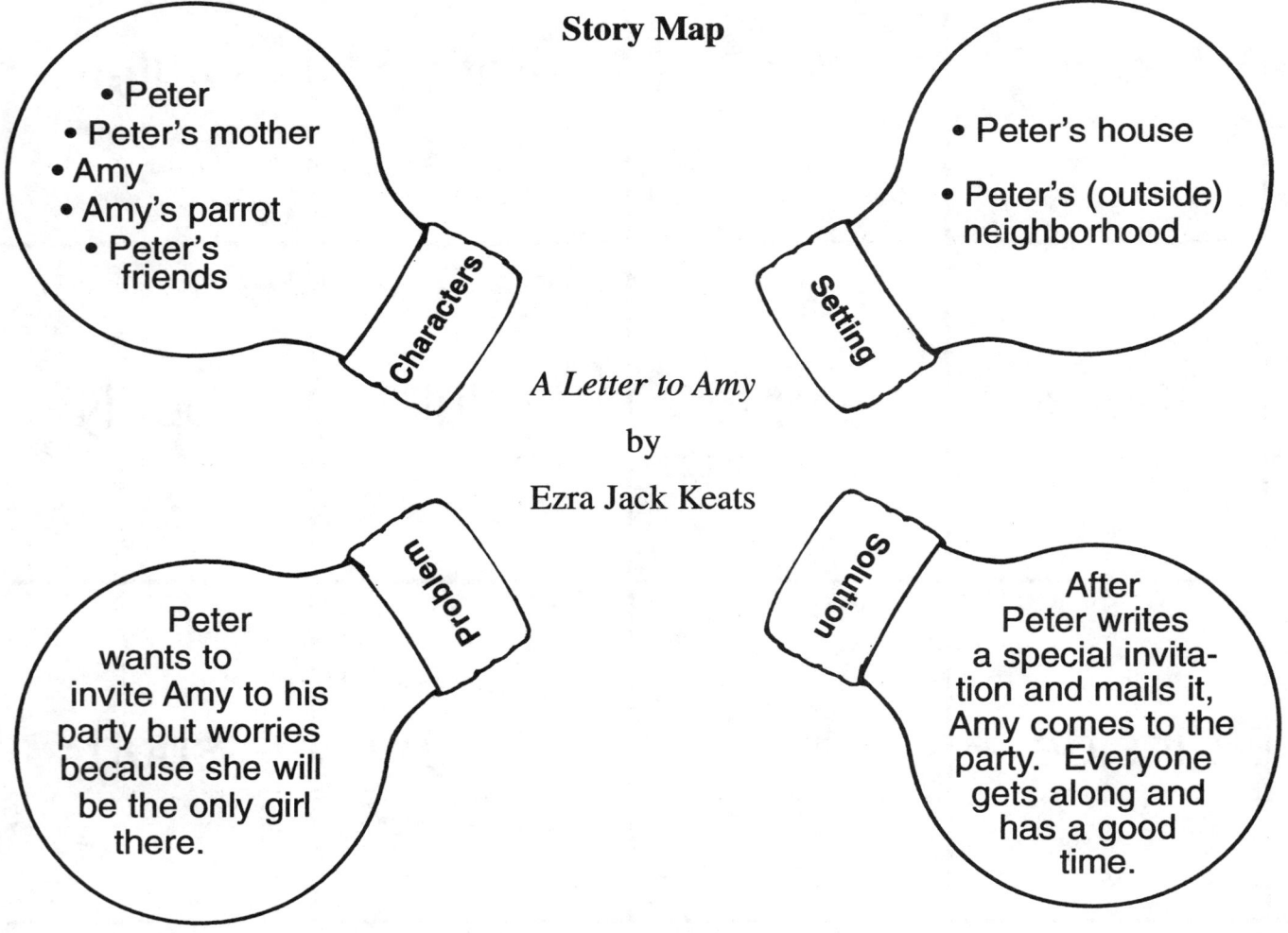

Characters
- Peter
- Peter's mother
- Amy
- Amy's parrot
- Peter's friends

Setting
- Peter's house
- Peter's (outside) neighborhood

A Letter to Amy

by

Ezra Jack Keats

Problem
Peter wants to invite Amy to his party but worries because she will be the only girl there.

Solution
After Peter writes a special invitation and mails it, Amy comes to the party. Everyone gets along and has a good time.

A Letter to Amy *(cont.)*

Before Reading the Book

Suggested introductory scripts and activities follow:

- Tell some ways that people let others know what they want or let them know about something special that is happening. (A list might include telling them, showing them, writing, calling, signals, etc.)

- When someone sends a message to someone else, it is called communication. Let's brainstorm and add to the list of ways people communicate. (talk, sing, write, smile, body language, telegraph, phone, TV, radio, words, signals, codes, signing, etc.)

- Have students tell how they would choose to communicate the following:

  —You want to thank your aunt for a gift, but she lives far away.
  —You are in school and need to go to the bathroom.
  —You want to let a new student know that you would like to be his friend.
  —You do not like what you are having for supper.
  —You are having a party and want others to come.

- Who can tell us what an invitation is? Discuss types of invitations and encourage students to tell about different ones they may have received or sent.

- If you were sending invitations for your birthday party, what information would you need to write them? What information would you need to send them in the mail? Describe what happens after you place a letter in the mailbox.

- Who has a favorite kind of weather? Let's name different kinds of weather and what each is like. (See pages 49 and 50).

Some New and Interesting Words from the Story

letter	mail	wind
writing	stamp	repeated
party	parrot	chased
birthday	reflection	clouds
sealed	flash	wish
envelope		

A Letter to Amy *(cont.)*

After Reading the Book

Suggested discussion topics and activities follow:

- Why do you think Peter decides to write to Amy instead of just calling or telling her about the party?

- Describe how you think Peter feels when the letter blows out of his hands. How do you think he feels when he grabs it and bumps into Amy? How is Amy feeling?

- If you were Amy in the story, would you go to Peter's party? Tell why or why not.

- If you were Peter, would you invite Amy?

- Write a pretend invitation to Peter or Amy, inviting him or her to your birthday party.

- After mailing the letter and finding out that Amy has run off crying, Peter worries that Amy will not come to his party. The story says Peter sees his reflection in the street, and it looks all mixed up. What is a reflection? Why is Peter's reflection mixed up? How do you think Peter is feeling right then, when his reflection is "mixed up"? (Help students think about the idea that Peter, himself, probably feels very mixed up about the situation.)

- Describe a time when you felt unsure or mixed up about something. What did you decide to do? How did it turn out?

- It starts to storm when Peter leaves his house to mail the letter. There are wind, rain, thunder, and lightning. Is weather helpful or harmful? Have students write sentences or paragraphs about their favorite kinds of weather. Illustrate them and bind them together for a classroom book about weather. (See pages 49 and 50.)

Category Coats

Write words from the umbrella onto the correct raincoats below.

This is called "grouping into correct categories."

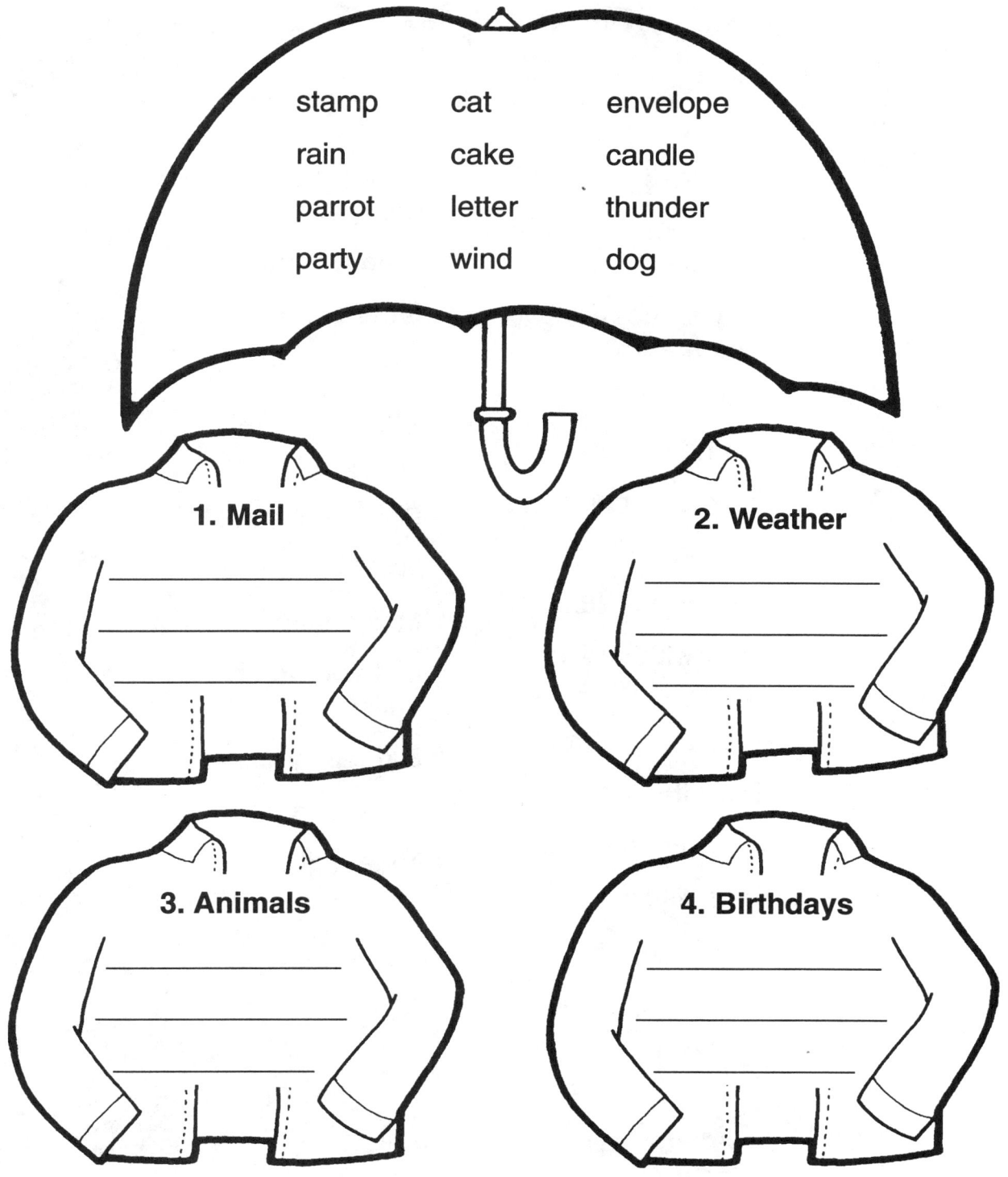

stamp   cat   envelope

rain   cake   candle

parrot   letter   thunder

party   wind   dog

1. Mail

2. Weather

3. Animals

4. Birthdays

Party Time!

Circle the things that you might do at a birthday party. Draw an X through the things you would not do at a party.

Eat cake.

Get your eyes checked.

Buy some milk and bread.

Win a prize.

Do homework.

Talk to a friend.

Change a flat tire.

Listen to a story.

Play with toys or games.

Kick or hit a friend.

Mow the lawn.

Blow out candles.

Be polite.

Play pin the tail on the donkey.

Sing a song.

Open a present.

Clean your room.

Enjoy ice cream.

Dance.

Draw a picture.

Watch a movie.

Mail a letter.

Get your tooth pulled.

Eat candy.

Take a bath.

Take a gift.

Weather Words

Below are six weather-related words and six weather pictures. Cut them out carefully. On the next page are six sentences. Paste the correct weather word over the word in the box so that the sentence makes sense. Then paste the correct weather picture beside that sentence.

Weather Words *(cont.)*

1. Wear your ⬜ swimsuit ⬜ today because it is raining.	
2. The ⬜ sun ⬜ blew the letter out of his hand.	
3. I like to splash in puddles of ⬜ snow ⬜ .	
4. I saw a very bright flash of ⬜ thunder ⬜ .	
5. It was so ⬜ sunny ⬜ this morning we couldn't see across the street.	
6. The ⬜ sleet ⬜ covered up the sun and blue sky.	

Worth Repeating

Color the parrot only if the two sentences *parrot* each other—that is, mean the same thing.

Sue is happy. Sue is glad.	
Bill has practice on Saturday. Bill's practice is the day after Monday.	
Before you color, fold the paper. Fold your paper first, before coloring it.	
We went shopping yesterday. The day before today we shopped.	
The black dog's collar is big. The big dog's collar is black.	
The TV program starts before lunch. That TV program is on in the morning.	
Amy came to the party late. Amy was not on time for the party.	

Writing Special Letters

An invitation is a special letter. Write a letter to a friend, inviting the friend to come to your house to play on Saturday. Make sure you tell your friend what time to come and any other important details.

Goggles!

Themes

- Friendship
- City Life
- Dealing with Difficult People
- Finding Things
- Help from Pets

Summary

Archie and Peter, two young friends, along with Peter's faithful dog Willie, are excited when they find a pair of goggles without lenses. Some bigger boys, however, try to take the goggles away, and a fight takes place. In the midst of the scuffle, Willie runs away with the goggles, and Archie and Peter get away to their secret hideout. With the help of their dog, some luck, and a clever plan, the younger boys outsmart the bullies and return safely home with their prized goggles.

Story Map

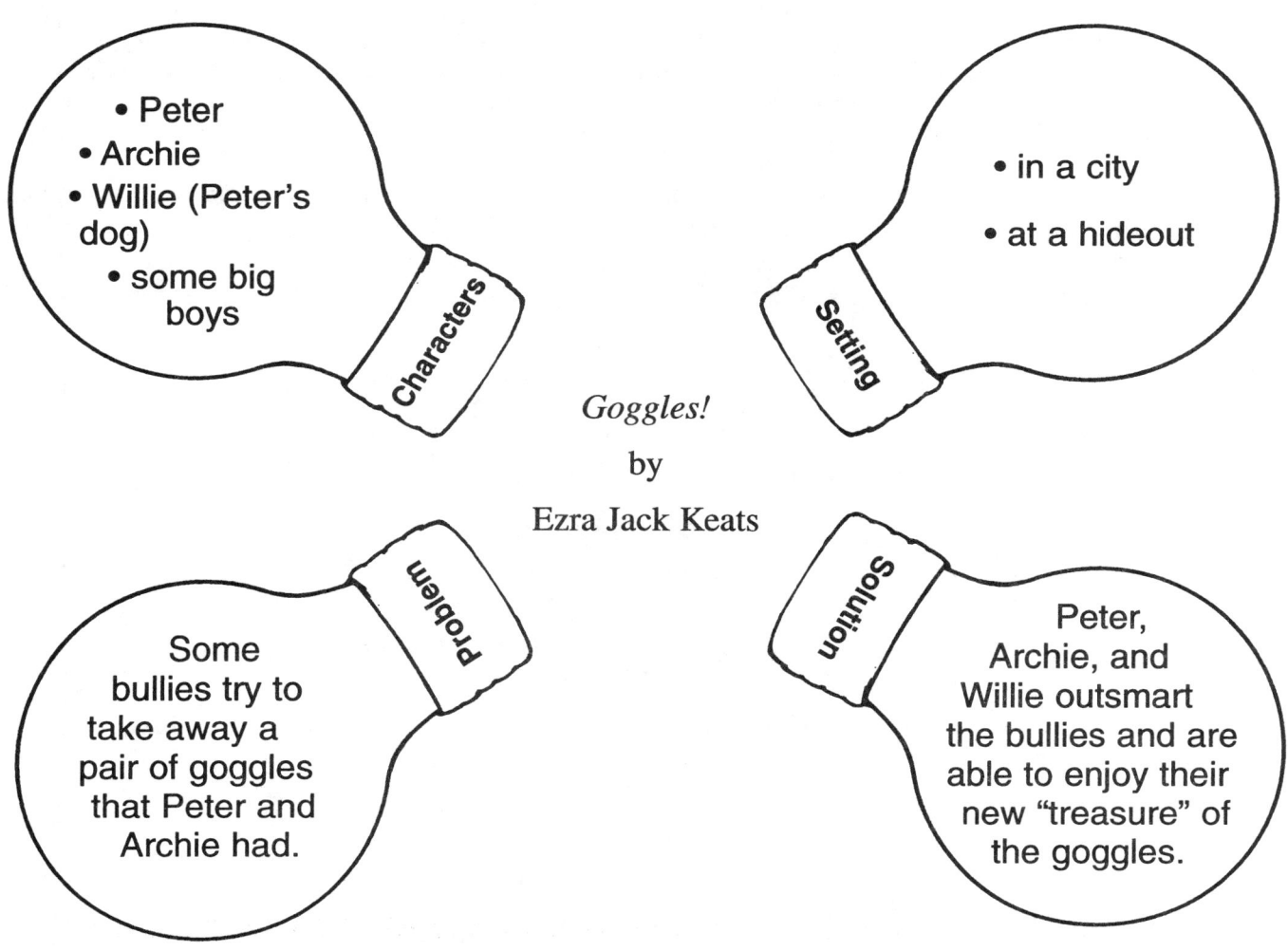

Characters
- Peter
- Archie
- Willie (Peter's dog)
- some big boys

Setting
- in a city
- at a hideout

Goggles!
by
Ezra Jack Keats

Problem
Some bullies try to take away a pair of goggles that Peter and Archie had.

Solution
Peter, Archie, and Willie outsmart the bullies and are able to enjoy their new "treasure" of the goggles.

Goggles! *(cont.)*

Before Reading the Book

Suggested introductory scripts and activities follow:

- Obtain a pair of old or lenseless goggles or sunglasses and show them to students. Invite students to tell what they would do with them if they found them lying on the ground.

- Share ideas about secret hideouts, forts, or special meeting places that friends often have. Discuss what makes these places special.

- Discuss differences between where children play in the city versus where they might play or what they might do in a more rural area. Contrast where they live to other cities, villages, or locations around you.

- Ask students if they have ever had an encounter with older, bigger, or bossier children who were intentionally mean to them. Discuss the term "bully." Invite them to share some incidents involving bullies, following up with talk about what characteristics and attributes make a person mean or unfriendly or unkind.

- Ask students about special tricks or brave deeds that their pets may have done. Perhaps the students can better relate to a television show or a book about a pet. Do they think pets can sense when their owners need something? Do they think pets can understand human actions or words?

- Have students tell about something unusual or unexpected they may have found. Perhaps it was a coin, some jewelry, or a toy left behind. Invite them to imagine something they might find that they would consider truly a treasure. (Make sure you discuss the issues and values with your students that surround finding lost objects or valuables that do not belong to them.)

Some New and Interesting Words from the Story

goggles	knocked	ground
appeared	through	fence
pocket	breath	hole
found	crept	fists
stared	hideout	footsteps

Goggles! *(cont.)*

After Reading the Book

Suggested discussion topics and activities follow:

- Peter and Archie live in a city. Look through the book again and describe what the city is like. Where do they play? Where do you think they would play if they lived in your town?

- Describe their hideout. How is it set up? What materials do they use to make their hideout? Tell what the pipe is used for. Do you have a hideout? (Complete the Secret Hideout sheet and use for a further discussion or journal or story-writing idea.)

- Archie and Peter are good friends. Describe them. Which friend is taller? Do they both wear glasses? Who does most of the talking? How do they work together to fool the older boys? (Complete the Friends sheet).

- If you had been Peter, would you have given the big boys the goggles? Do you think that Peter or Archie are scared? What might the bigger boys have done if they had caught Peter, Archie, or Willie?

- What would you do if you were stopped by someone after school who demanded you give them something? Have you ever been in a scary or dangerous situation before?

- Use the pattern for students to make their own goggles from tagboard or heavy construction paper. Role play various parts of the story with the goggles.

- Using the student's self-made goggles or an old pair of goggles, play a game similar to "Duck, Duck, Goose," which now becomes "Goggle Goose." The pair of goggles are dropped behind a child sitting in the circle and must be put on before the "goggled goose" can run after the other person!

Friends

In the story, Archie and Peter are good friends. Below are several statements about friends. If you agree with the statement, color the happy face. If you disagree with the statement, color the sad face.

Statement	Agree	Disagree
Friends share their toys.	☺	☹
Friends hit each other.	☺	☹
Friends will help each other.	☺	☹
Friends can make you feel better.	☺	☹
Friends make you feel lonely.	☺	☹
Friends try to hurt your feelings.	☺	☹
You can share special times with a friend.	☺	☹
Friends play together.	☺	☹
Friends argue and don't try to get along.	☺	☹
Friends don't care about you.	☺	☹
Friends are important.	☺	☹
You would feel sad if your friend got sick or hurt.	☺	☹
Write one of your own:	☺	☹

Magic Goggles

Use an old pair of sunglasses or goggles. (You may want to remove the lenses.) Have students sit in a circle on the floor. The "magic goggles" are passed around the circle so that each child has a chance to put them on. When it is a student's turn to wear the goggles, he/she must make one positive or complimentary comment to another student in the circle.

Each time a student passes the goggles to the next student, the following verse may be said together by all the students:

> "GOGGLES, MAGIC GOGGLES,
> NOW TELL US WHAT YOU SEE;
> TELL ME SOMETHING SPECIAL
> THAT YOU CAN SAY OF ME!"

Explain to the students that what they choose to say about another student should be something true, and that nothing negative or hurtful can be said. Initiate a discussion around the idea that everyone has something positive about them. Possibly brainstorm or make a written list of positive attributes before the activity.

Examples of what a child may say to another when it is his/her turn to wear the magic goggles could be somewhat like the following:

- "I like the way Mary is always smiling."

- "Johnny always lets others borrow a pencil when they can't find their own."

- "Something special about Jenny is that she keeps on trying at math, even when it's really hard."

Depending on the age of the students, you may wish to determine a set pattern or draw names ahead of time as to which student has something positive said about him/her. This ensures that all students will get at least one turn.

Variation: Before this activity, give students three self-sticking mini-notes, blank white labels, or paper with tape. Ask them to think of three good qualities about people and write each on one of the pieces of paper. Then, during the "Magic Goggles" activity, the student wearing the goggles can walk over to another student and "pin" the word onto his/her shirt as well as say the positive quality or thought about the other student.

Encourage students to discuss how they feel when someone says something nice about them. Assign "homework" to the students that involves going home and telling family members something nice about each one. This also makes an excellent idea for journal writing.

Compound Word Goggles

Match the word parts from the box to form compound words.

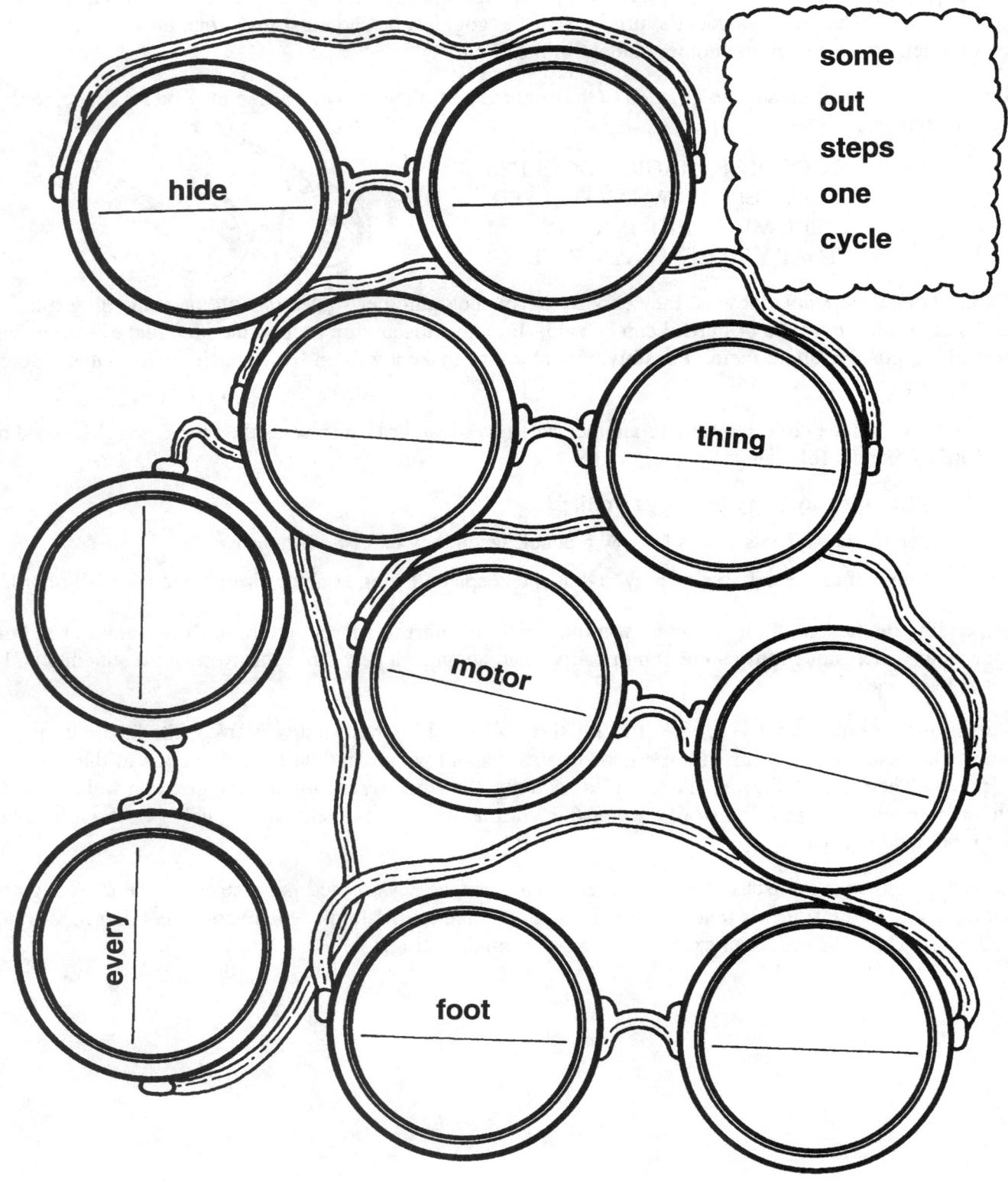

some
out
steps
one
cycle

hide

thing

motor

every

foot

Feelings

Think about the story and how the boys feel at different times. Fill in each blank with a word that tells the feeling.

Word Bank

mean   proud   scared
happy   brave

1. When Peter finds the goggles, he feels _____ .

2. When the big boys try to take the goggles, they are being _____ .

3. Peter is _____ to stand up to the bigger boys.

4. Archie feels _____ when Peter puts up his fists.

5. When Peter and Archie fool the bigger boys, they feel _____ .

Your Feelings

Finish each sentence about your feelings:

1. I feel happy when _____ .

2. I feel scared when _____ .

3. I feel brave when _____ .

4. I am mean when _____ .

5. I feel proud_____ .

I feel _____

_____

Secret Hideout

Like Peter and Archie in the story, many people have secret or special places.

❑ Do you have a secret hideout or a special place? _____

❑ Who goes there? _____

_____

❑ When do you go there? _____

_____

❑ Where is your special place? _____

_____

❑ What is it like there? _____

_____

Draw a picture below of your secret hideout or special place.

Pattern for Goggles

1. Trace the pattern on tagboard or heavy construction paper.

2. Decorate and cut out your goggles.

3. Punch out the holes and tie with rug yarn or cord.

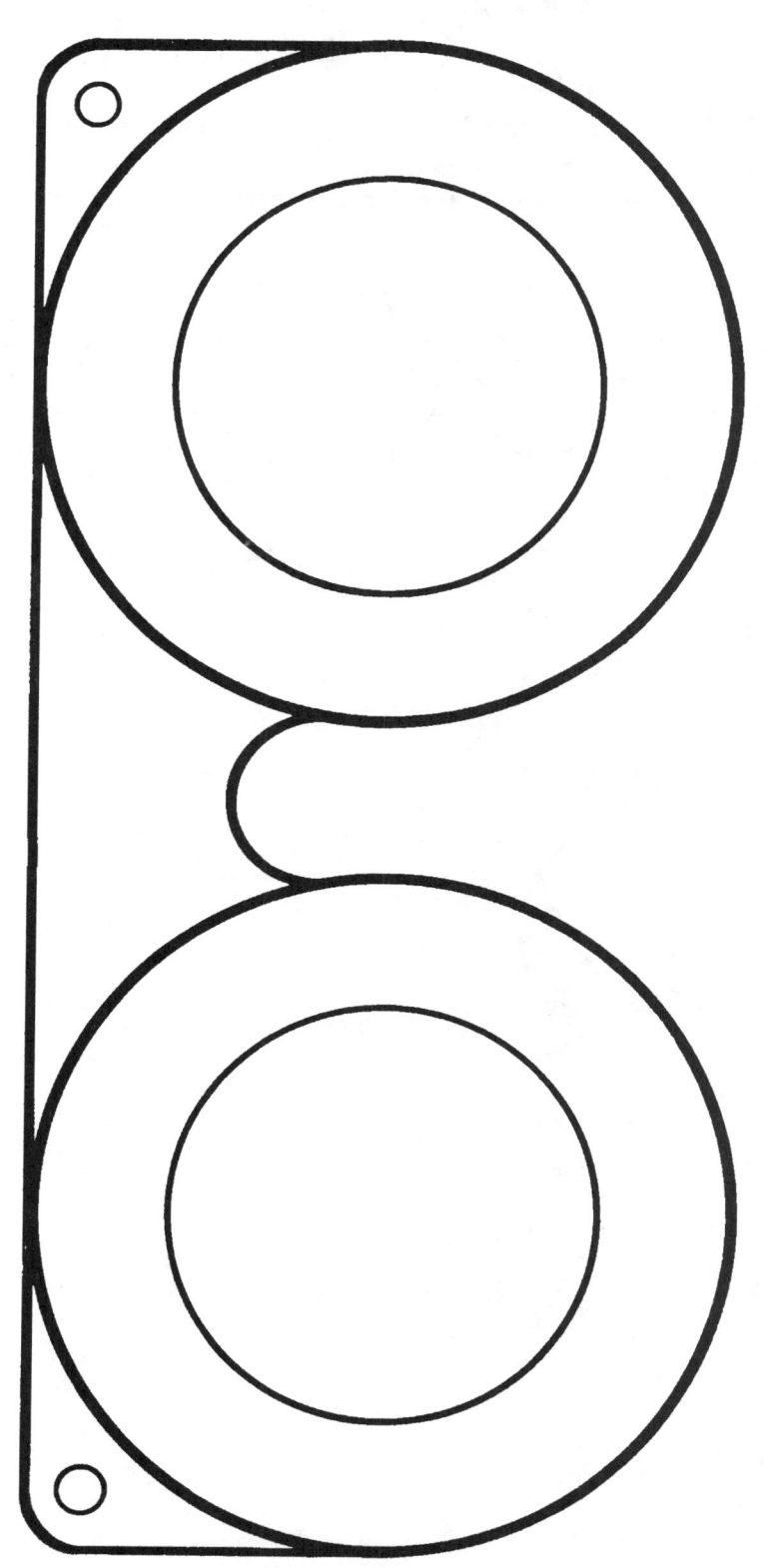

Hi, Cat!

> **Themes**
> - Animal Friends
> - Stray Animals
> - Pets
> - How Animals Show Affection

Summary

On his way to meet his friend Peter, Archie sees a cat that he has never seen before, and he says "hi" to it. To his surprise and at times frustration, the cat takes a liking to Archie and follows him through the neighborhood. The cat ruins a show that Archie and Peter put on for their other friends. Archie complains about the cat and tells his mother about it, but he feels rather good about the cat liking him and even following him home.

Story Map

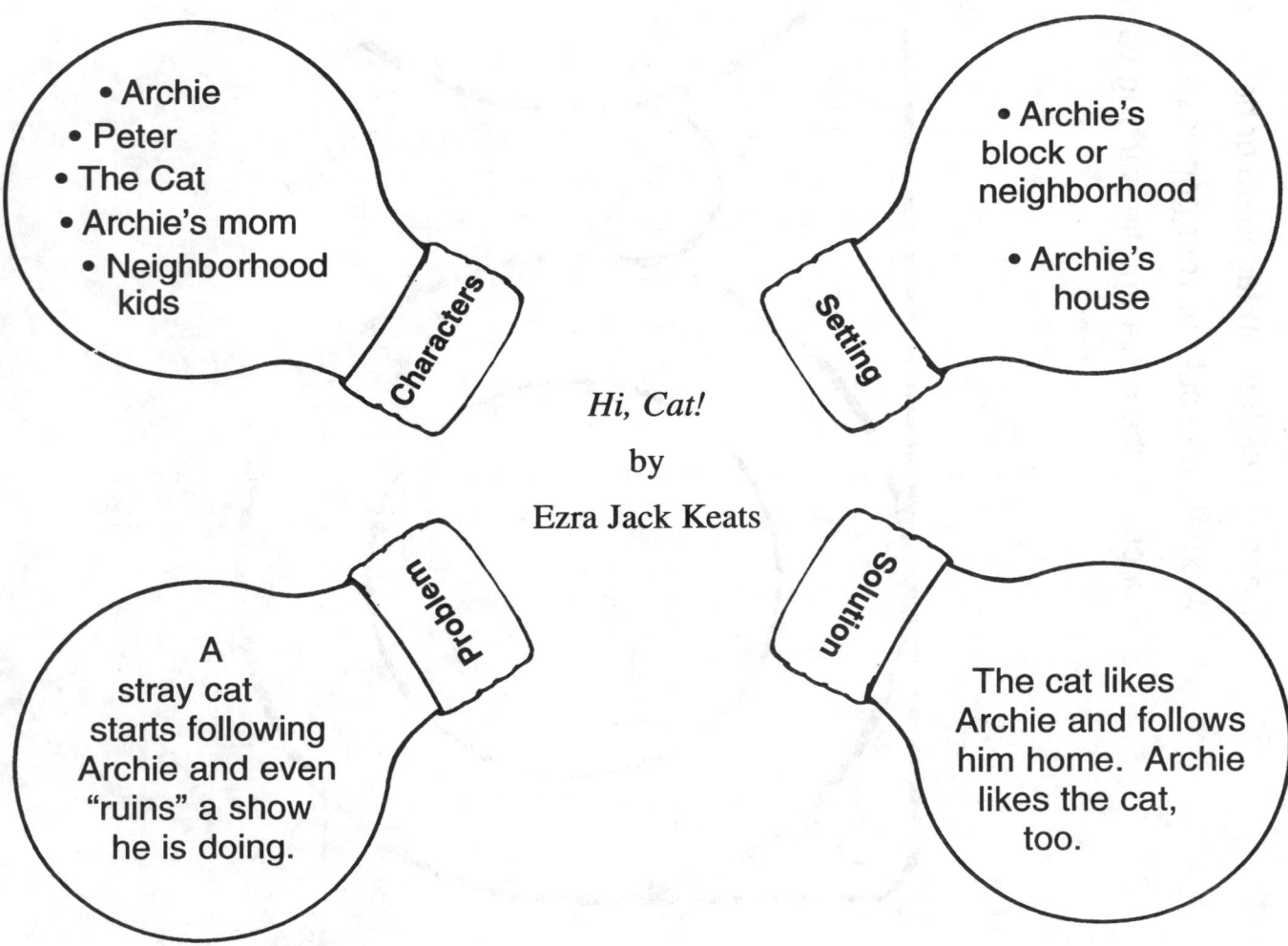

Characters
- Archie
- Peter
- The Cat
- Archie's mom
- Neighborhood kids

Setting
- Archie's block or neighborhood
- Archie's house

Hi, Cat!

by

Ezra Jack Keats

Problem

A stray cat starts following Archie and even "ruins" a show he is doing.

Solution

The cat likes Archie and follows him home. Archie likes the cat, too.

62

Hi, Cat! *(cont.)*

Before Reading the Book

Suggested introductory scripts and activities follow:

- Who knows what a "stray" is, or what a stray animal is? Has anyone ever taken home a stray cat or dog or other animal and fed it or made it a pet?

- Why do animals sometimes follow people around? Why will a dog come meet you or a cat jump into your lap? Tell about the last time an animal followed you around.

- Sometimes friends or neighbors get together to entertain each other. Have any of you ever put on a show or an act for friends or family?

- In the story *Hi, Cat!,* Archie and Peter try to put on a show for their friends, but it gets ruined. What kinds of things could happen to spoil a show?

- Make a list of special talents or things you could do if you were in a show or if you put on an act for someone else. (e.g., singing, dancing, telling jokes, juggling, etc.)

- Write the following statement on the board:

Cats are   animals!

- Now, let's think of as many different words as we can that could fill in the blank to describe what cats are like. (e.g., nice, friendly, clever, quiet, etc.)

- Describe how cats are different from dogs or other types of pets.

- What things do all pets need in order to stay alive?

Some New and Interesting Words from the Story

waited	giggled	closer
voice	licked	thought
grown	respect	shake
block	surprise	shook
reflection	appeared	mustache
		laughing

Hi, Cat! *(cont.)*

After Reading the Book

Suggested discussion topics and activities follow:

- Who is Archie going to meet? Why?

- When Archie sees the cat, he says "Hi, Cat!" What do you think Archie's voice sounds like when he says that?

- Let's say "Hi, Cat!" several times and make our voices sound different each time. First say it shyly. Try sounding angry, excited, and scared. Sometimes our voices can give others a clue as to how we are feeling or what we are thinking.

  (Try other sentences or phrases using various voice inflections. Discuss tone, expression, and inflection in verbal communication.)

- When Archie is pretending to be old like a grandpa, how does his voice sound?

- How does he walk?

- How does he look?

- Willie licks Archie's mustache off, and Archie says, "No respect for old age." Who can tell us what respect is? (See page 70 for related activity.)

- Why do you think Archie's mom tells him that he is well rid of a cat like that? Do you think the cat likes Archie or just wants some food?

- How do animals show that they like a person?

- Name three things that your pet does to show that it loves you and your family.

Sense or Nonsense?

Circle YES or NO to answer each question:

1. Could a stray cat follow you home?   YES   NO
2. Could a stray elephant come to your house for dinner?   YES   NO
3. Could you see your reflection in a store window?   YES   NO
4. Could a man grow a mustache out of ice cream?   YES   NO
5. Could you put on a show for your friends?   YES   NO
6. Could a cat dance on a frog?   YES   NO
7. Could a dog be taller than a building?   YES   NO
8. Could a dog chase a cat?   YES   NO
9. Could a cat tear a paper bag?   YES   NO
10. Could a cat play the violin?   YES   NO
11. Could ice cream be green?   YES   NO
12. Could ice cream be hot?   YES   NO
13. Could a friend wait for you?   YES   NO
14. Can a wall walk?   YES   NO
15. Could a dog jump?   YES   NO
16. Could a horse jump?   YES   NO

❑ Write a real sentence of your own that makes sense:

_____

_____

❑ Write a nonsense sentence of your own:

_____

_____

Name That Pair!

Write the pair of related words from each sentence:

1. Willie the dog chased the cat.

   Name the animal pair: _____ , _____

2. Archie waited for Peter.

   Name the pair of friends: _____ , _____

3. Archie croaked and Susie giggled.

   Name the pair of sounds: _____ , _____

4. The big dog looked very tall.

   Name the pair of size words: _____ , _____

5. We had ice cream and cake and played games at the party.

   Name the pair of desserts: _____ , _____

6. Grandpa winked when the cat meowed at Grandma.

   Name the pair of relatives: _____ , _____

7. Archie's hand came out of the puppet's ear.

   Name the body parts: _____ , _____

8. The black cat chased the brown cat.

   Name the pair of colors: _____ , _____

9. He put the book in a bag.

   Name a pair made of paper: _____ , _____

10. His hat and sweater were green and blue.

    Name the pair of clothes: _____ , _____

Root Words and Endings

Cut out the cones from this page and the scoops of ice cream from the next page. Match the root words with the words used from the story

Optional: When you have all 10 ice cream cones matched, choose five of the words and write them in original sentences on your paper.

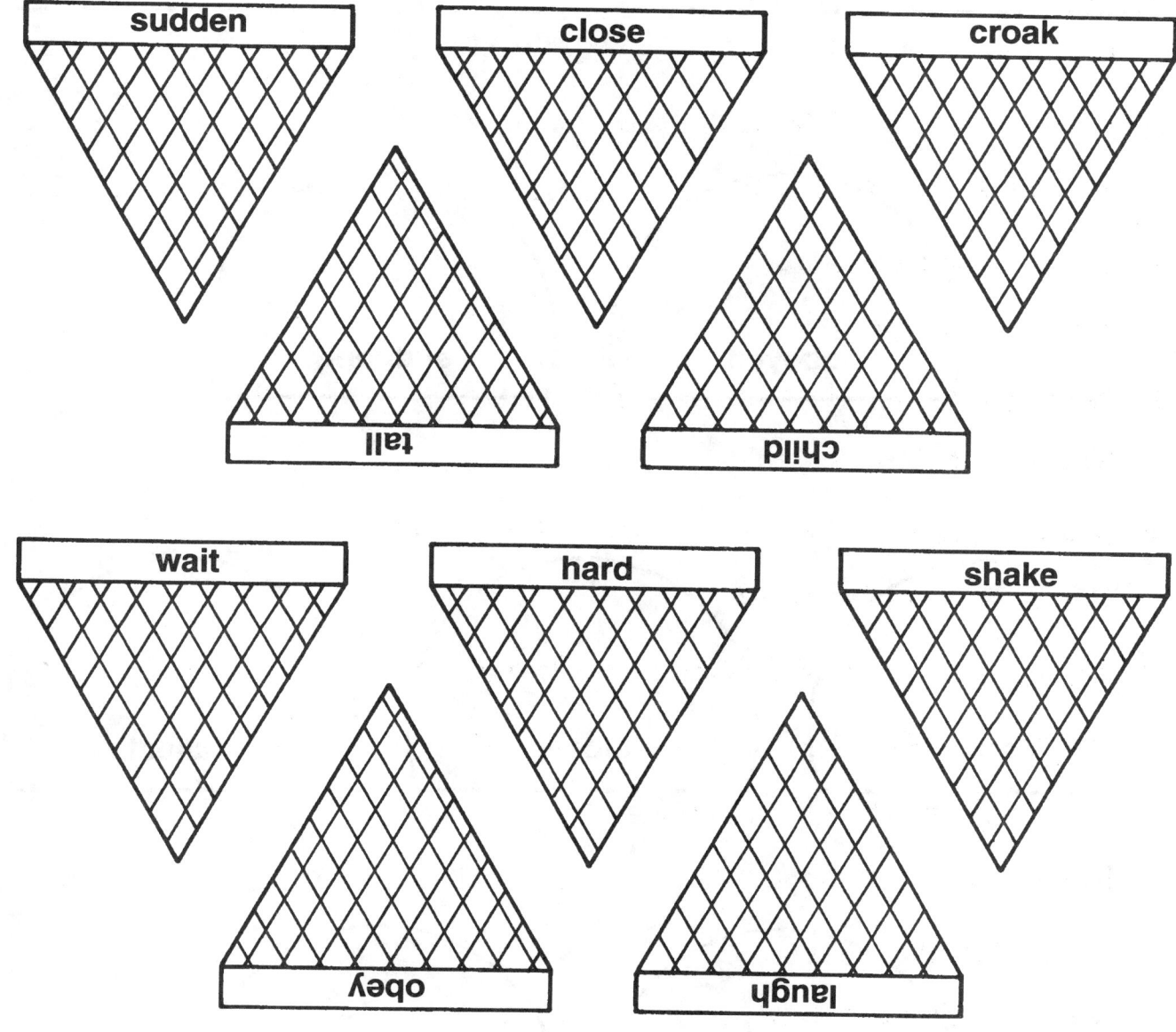

Root Words and Endings *(cont.)*

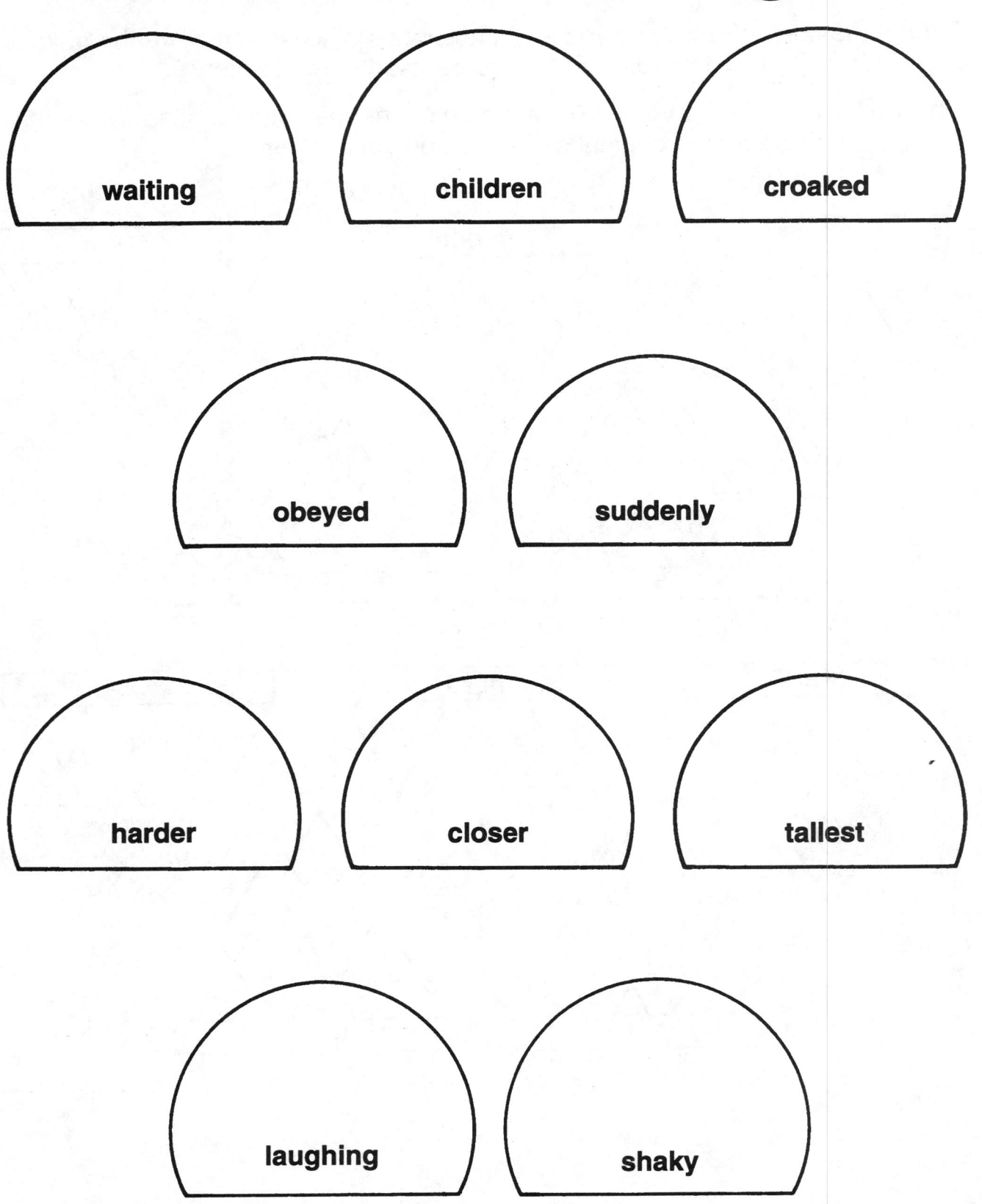

waiting

children

croaked

obeyed

suddenly

harder

closer

tallest

laughing

shaky

Animal Actions

Circle the verbs (or action words) in each sentence.

1. That cat purred when she walked by.
2. His dog wagged his tail.
3. The brown cat meowed softly.
4. The horse nuzzled his head against my hand.
5. Kitty jumped up on Mom's lap.
6. His ears perked up when he heard me.
7. The puppy ran after the boy.
8. The gerbil raced around his cage.
9. The dog barked at the stranger.
10. He growled at the mailman.

Write the names of six animals from above:

_____   _____

_____   _____

_____   _____

Write each verb below without an ending:

Example: purred   **purr**

wagged _____   nuzzled _____

meowed _____   jumped _____

perked _____   raced _____

Showing Respect

Showing respect means showing others that you care about who they are and what they think or feel. Respect lets another person know that you think that person is important.

If the statement tells a traditional way we can show respect for another person, circle the letter in the first column. If it does not show respect or is disrespectful, circle the letter in column two.

Statement	Respect	Disrespect
1. Talk back to adults and teachers.	P	H
2. Be careful and gentle with all living things.	A	R
3. Lie to someone.	T	V
4. Hold the door open for another.	E	S
5. Stand up to salute the American flag when it goes by.	R	L
6. Get into someone else's desk without asking.	G	E
7. Interrupt when someone else is talking.	B	S
8. In a crowded room or bus, let an older person sit down.	P	J
9. Talk and fool around during a quiet movie or program.	H	E
10. Take your hat off in a building or restaurant.	C	K
11. Burp out loud.	M	T

Write the circled letters below to spell out a secret message:

___ ___ ___ ___   ___ ___ ___ ___ ___ ___ ___

The Alphabetical Cat

Write the following words in alphabetical order on the cat.

store	mustache	looked	corner	obeyed
voice	block	tallest	paper	world

1. _____

2. _____

3. _____

4. _____

5. _____

6. _____

7. _____

8. _____

9. _____

10. _____

Apartment Three

Themes
- Apartment Living
- Music and Emotions
- Neighbors
- New Friends

Summary

Sam and his family live in an apartment building in the city. One rainy afternoon Sam hears the harmonica music he so often hears. He decides this time to find out where it is coming from. With his little brother Ben, he checks out each apartment on each floor of the building. Quite by chance the boys meet the blind man living in apartment three. He plays the harmonica and plays special music for Sam. The music brings out special feelings for Sam. The boys invite the blind man to take a walk with them the next day. The music and their new friend make them feel very happy.

Story Map

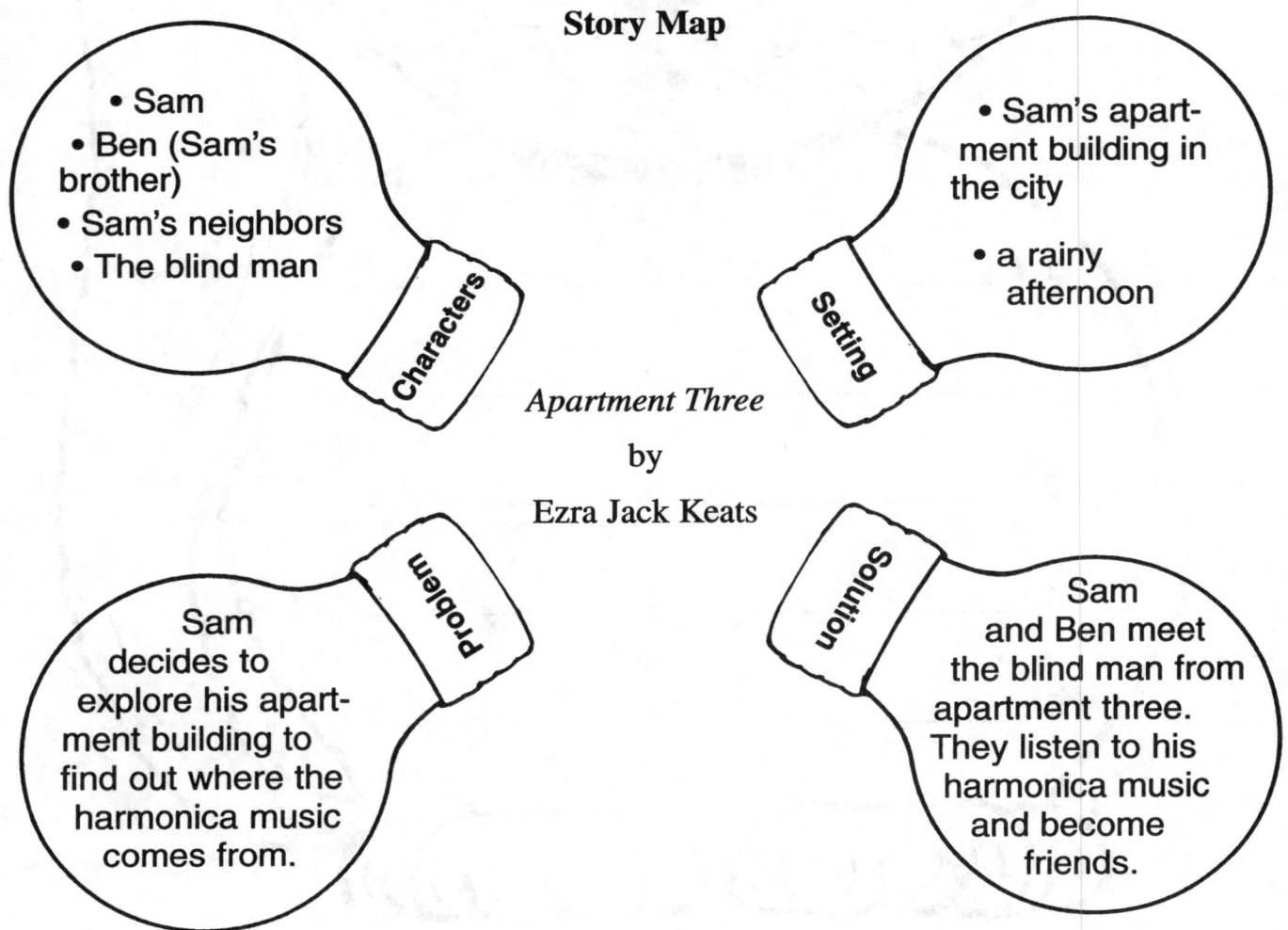

Characters
- Sam
- Ben (Sam's brother)
- Sam's neighbors
- The blind man

Setting
- Sam's apartment building in the city
- a rainy afternoon

Apartment Three

by

Ezra Jack Keats

Problem

Sam decides to explore his apartment building to find out where the harmonica music comes from.

Solution

Sam and Ben meet the blind man from apartment three. They listen to his harmonica music and become friends.

Apartment Three *(cont.)*

Before Reading the Book

Suggested introductory scripts and activities follow:

- What is an apartment or an apartment building? How is an apartment different from a house or a trailer?

- Would you probably find more apartment buildings in the country, in a small town or village, or in a city?

- Who likes music? Name some different types of music or different instruments or ways to make music. Who plays an instrument? (Make a chart or graph of students' favorite kinds of music or instruments. Invite some students to bring in instruments and play for the class).

- Can music ever tell a story or tell how someone is feeling? (Discuss musicals, operas, ballets, or symphonies, and discuss how some musical pieces were composed to describe a story.)

- Play short excerpts from various kinds of music and ask students to tell how that particular piece makes them feel or what that type of music stands for. (This is an excellent activity to correlate with the music teacher and music lessons.)

- Discuss with your students what a sense is. List the five senses (seeing, hearing, touching, tasting, smelling) on a chart and name the body organs used with each sense. Discuss disabilities involving the senses, in particular what it means to be blind.

- Who knows what a "super" of an apartment building is? What does the word *superintendent* mean? Are there other kinds of superintendents? What do they do?

Some New and Interesting Words from the Story

rain	lonely	smells
against	music	family
sounds	floated	apartment
city	blind	played
building	sights	
harmonica	sounds	

Apartment Three (cont.)

After Reading the Book

Suggested discussion topics and activities follow:

- What do you think makes Sam want to go find out where the music is coming from?

- What is a harmonica? How is it played?

- Have students make their own "harmonicas" by cutting waxed paper and placing it over a comb and humming into it.

- If you had a choice, would you live in the city or country? Would you live in a house or an apartment building or some place different?

- If you lived in a tall apartment building, would you prefer to live on the first, second, or a higher floor? Why?

- In the story, the man in apartment three is blind. If he is blind, how does he know so much? (How does he know Sam likes Betsy, about the boys, what others are cooking or arguing about, about others' feelings and secrets?)

- After asking for a volunteer for this activity, use a heavy blindfold to cover the student's eyes. Have the student describe what it feels like not to be able to see. Can the "blind" student tell what others are doing around him anyway? Have others do things or make sounds or take the "blind" student for a walk. How can that student "sense" what is going on around him? Discuss how all our senses work together!

- In the story, what do you think it means when the blind man plays "purples, grays, rain, and smoke, and sounds of night" on his harmonica?

- When and why does his music change to fill the room up with "wild and happy" music? Do you think the blind man will go for a walk with the two boys? Do you think the three of them will become friends?

- Why do you suppose the blind man can play the harmonica so well? Do you think he enjoys music?

- While going through their apartment building, the boys hear a dog barking in apartment nine. Why do you think they feel the dog is mean? Is a dog's bark always mean? If the dog has a mean bark, what might the dog look like? Do we sometimes judge things or decide things using only one or some of our senses?

- Discuss the old sayings: "Looks can be deceiving," and "You can't tell a book by its cover." List other sayings that apply to this idea.

Doorway Word Search

Find the 14 words hidden in the top part of the door and circle them. Then write them in alphabetical order:

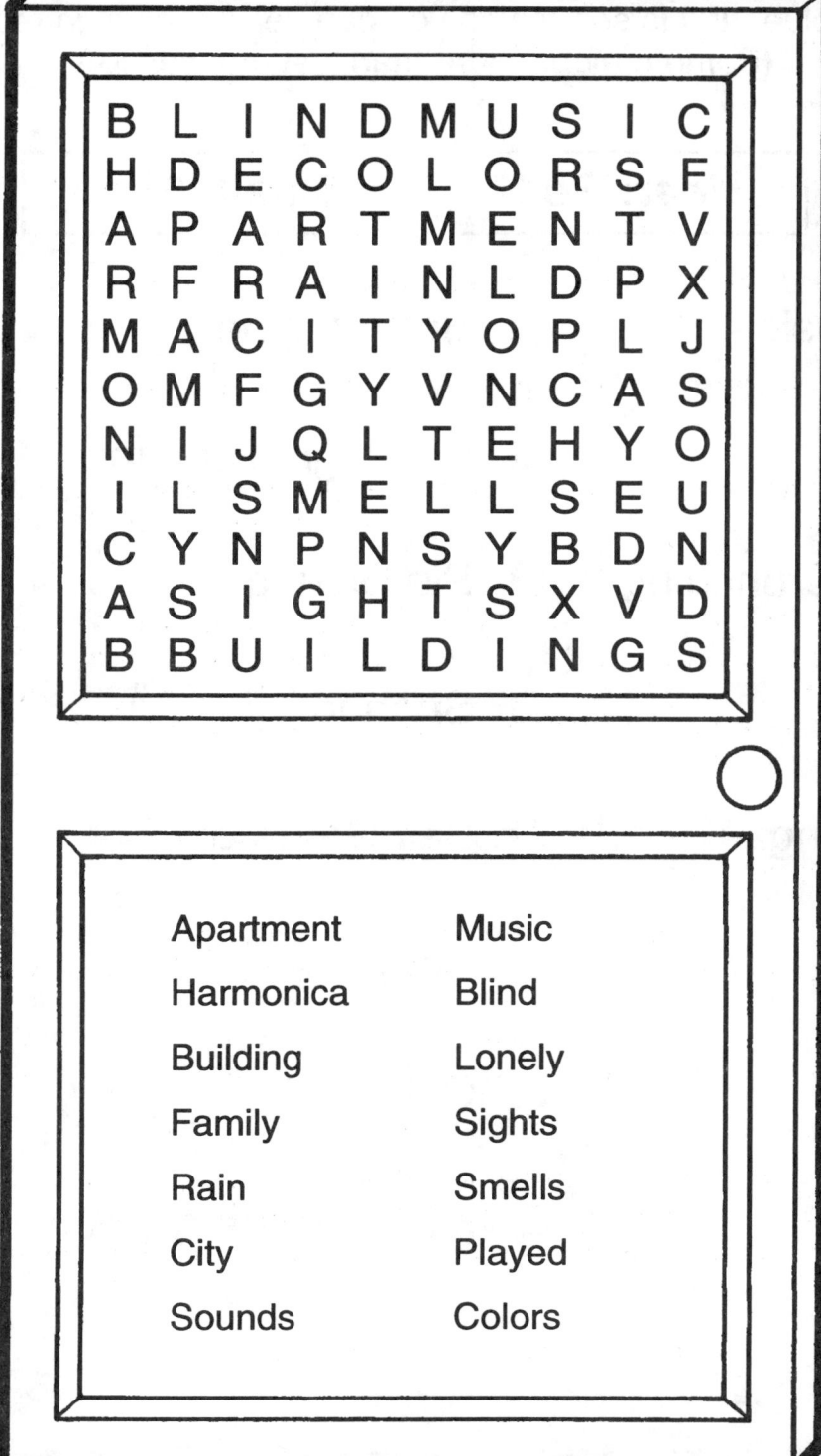

```
B L I N D M U S I C
H D E C O L O R S F
A P A R T M E N T V
R F R A I N L D P X
M A C I T Y O P L J
O M F G Y V N C A S
N I J Q L T E H Y O
I L S M E L L S E U
C Y N P N S Y B D N
A S I G H T S X V D
B B U I L D I N G S
```

Apartment   Music

Harmonica   Blind

Building   Lonely

Family   Sights

Rain   Smells

City   Played

Sounds   Colors

ABC Order:

1. _____

2. _____

3. _____

4. _____

5. _____

6. _____

7. _____

8. _____

9. _____

10. _____

11. _____

12. _____

13. _____

14. _____

Sights, Sounds, and Smells in the City

Which of the things listed below can you see, hear, or smell? If it is something that you can see, circle it in blue. If it is something you can hear, circle it in red. If it is a smell, circle it in green. (Some may be more than just one sense.)

See: Blue	**Hear:** Red	**Smell:** Green

- ❑ Harmonica Music
- ❑ Rain
- ❑ Potato Chips Crunching
- ❑ Cigarettes
- ❑ A Family Arguing
- ❑ Dog Barking
- ❑ Dog Sleeping
- ❑ Crying Baby

- ❑ Soft Singing
- ❑ Hall Light Broken
- ❑ Pie Baking
- ❑ Snoring
- ❑ Ball Game on TV
- ❑ Snowing
- ❑ Colors
- ❑ Milk Outside a Door

Favorite Senses

Finish each sentence to make it true.

❏ My favorite thing to **see** is _____

_____

_____

_____

❏ My favorite thing to **hear** is _____

_____

_____

_____

❏ My favorite thing to **smell** is _____

_____

_____

_____

❏ My favorite thing to **taste** is _____

_____

_____

_____

❏ My favorite thing to **touch** is _____

_____

_____

_____

City or Country?

Write each item in the box that tells where you would be most likely to see it or find it:

- ❏ cows in a pasture
- ❏ tall apartment buildings
- ❏ subways
- ❏ fields of corn
- ❏ tractors plowing
- ❏ restaurants
- ❏ movie houses
- ❏ many stores/factories
- ❏ barns & silos
- ❏ big open gardens
- ❏ horses in a field
- ❏ busy streets

City	Country

Who Lives Where?

Cut apart each strip that describes who lives in each apartment and match it with the correctly numbered apartment door on the next page.

You may need to look back in the book and reread certain pages to help you find who is in each apartment.

A. the "super" of the apartment building

B. loud, juicy snoring and a new mattress

C. big Mr. Muntz, crunching on potato chips

D. a mother singing softly to her crying baby

E. Betsy

F. smells of cigarettes, cooking, and a family arguing

G. not a sound from this apartment

H. ball game on TV sounding like a million people cheering

I. more yelling from this apartment

J. Sam and Ben live in this apartment.

K. a really mean, barking dog

L. a quiet apartment with milk sitting outside the door

Who Lives Where? *(cont.)*

Cut the 12 apartment doors apart and match them with the strips from the preceding page that tell who lives in each apartment.

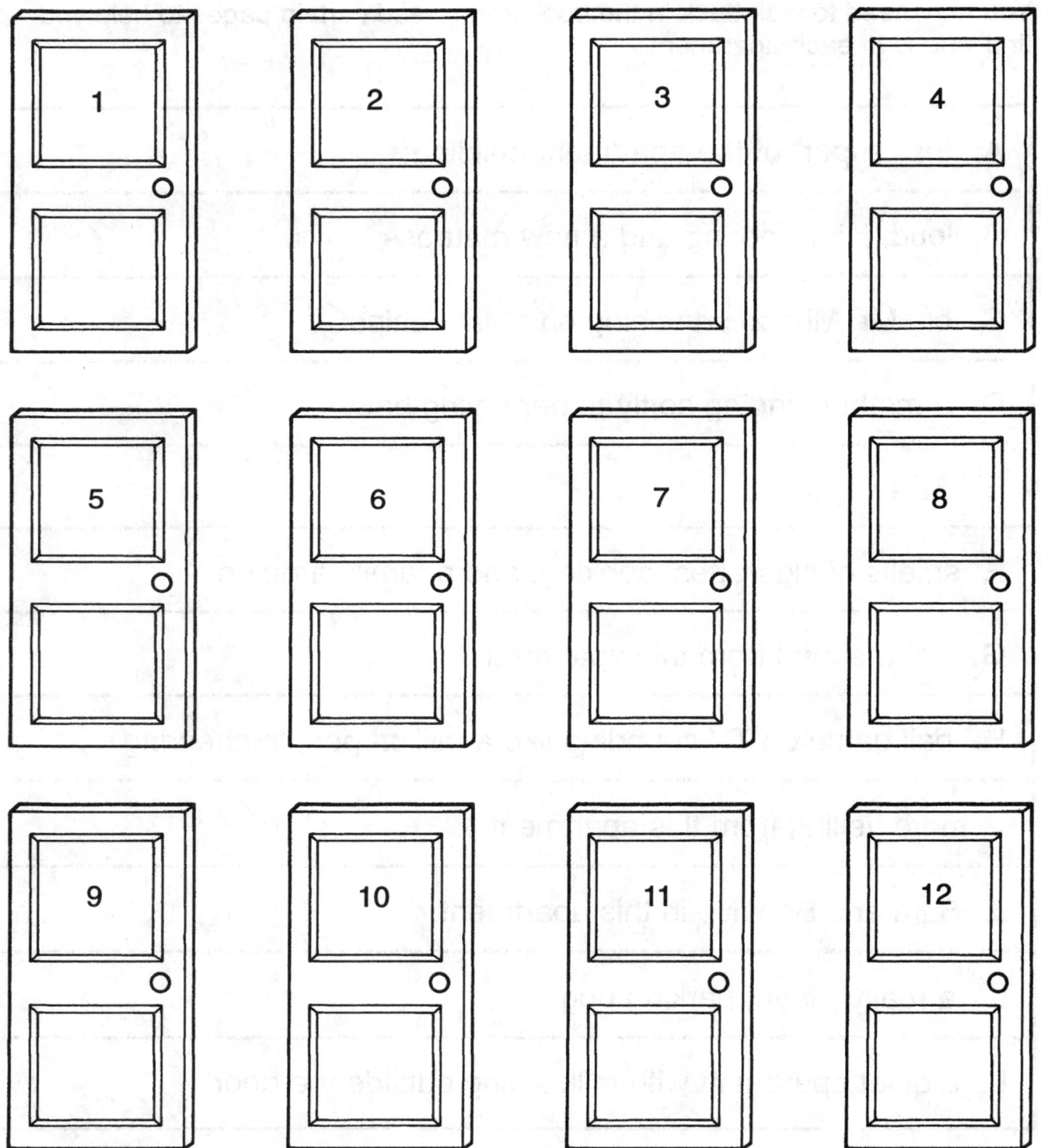

Pet Show!

Themes

- Pets
- Neighborhoods
- Love of Animals
- Regard for Others

Summary

There is a pet show taking place in Archie's neighborhood. Archie decides to enter his cat, but when he looks for the cat it is nowhere to be found. All his friends help him look for the cat before the pet show starts. The cat eventually shows up with an older lady. Meanwhile, Archie comes up with a clever idea so he can still enter a "pet" in the show. The woman gets a blue ribbon for the cat with the longest whiskers. Archie's invisible pet, a germ in a jar, also wins a blue ribbon. After the show the woman tells Archie that she knows the cat is his and offers him the cat's blue ribbon. Archie makes the woman happy by letting her keep that ribbon!

Story Map

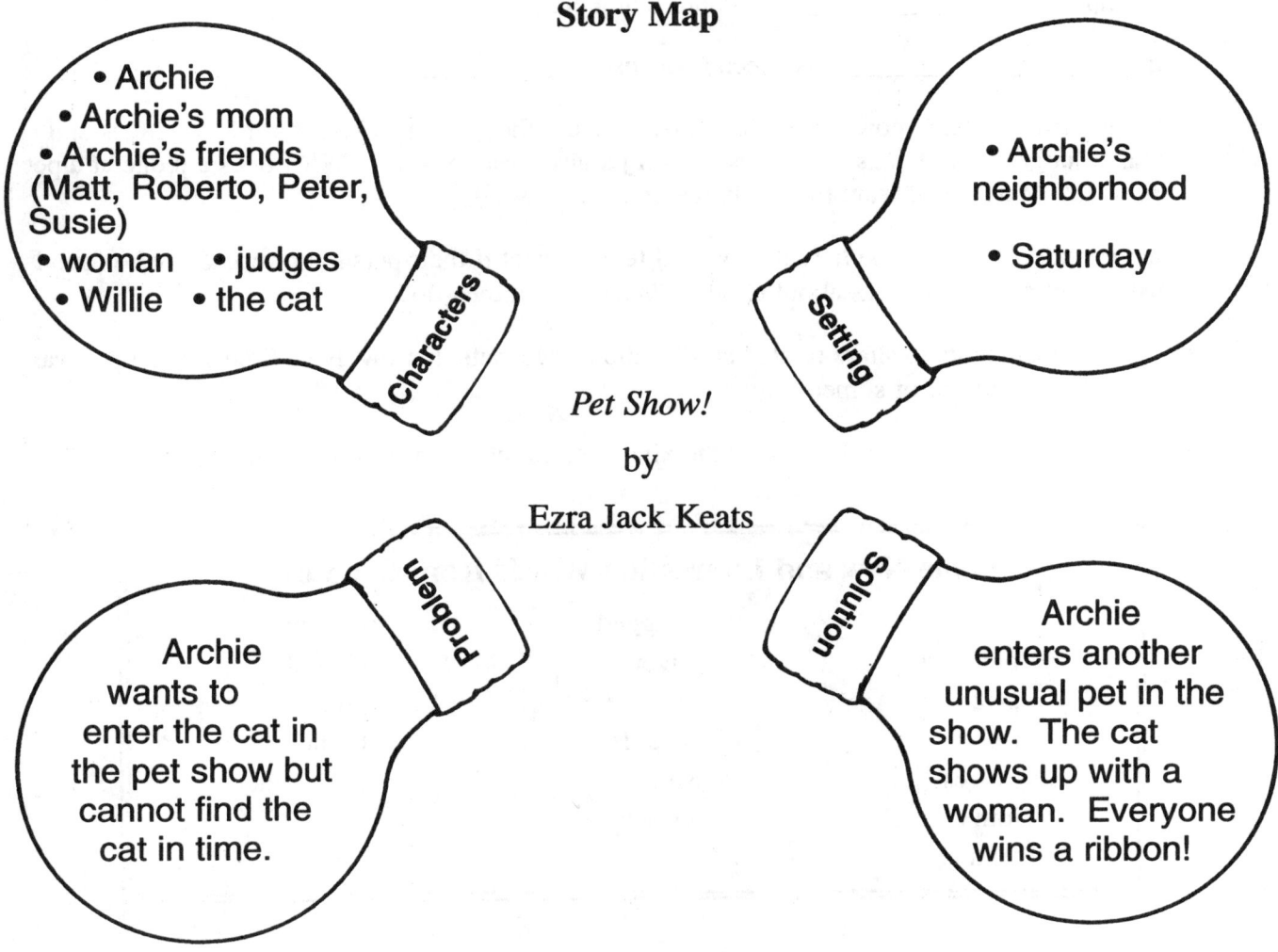

Characters
- Archie
- Archie's mom
- Archie's friends (Matt, Roberto, Peter, Susie)
- woman
- Willie
- judges
- the cat

Setting
- Archie's neighborhood
- Saturday

Pet Show!

by

Ezra Jack Keats

Problem

Archie wants to enter the cat in the pet show but cannot find the cat in time.

Solution

Archie enters another unusual pet in the show. The cat shows up with a woman. Everyone wins a ribbon!

Pet Show! *(cont.)*

Before Reading the Book

Suggested introductory scripts and activities follow:

- Who has ever heard of or been to a pet show? What is a pet show? What is it like?

- Name some of the different kinds of pets or animals you might see at a pet show. What is the most unusual pet you have ever seen at a pet show?

- If you had a pet show in your neighborhood or at your school, what pet would you enter in the pet show? For what might your pet be able to win a prize?

- Have students draw pictures of their pets or any pets they might take to a pet show. To go along with their pictures, have the students write several sentences or a paragraph describing their pets. Have students share their drawings and descriptions. You may want to prepare a story/sentence sheet for younger students to use.

  Example: My _____ would win a prize for _____ .

  or: My _____ is special because _____ .

- Ask students if they know what a judge is. Discuss the idea of different kinds of judges and what a judge does. Focus the discussion on judges for a pet show. What does a judge at a pet show do? Would you want to be a judge at a pet show?

- Invite students to imagine how they would feel or react if their pets hid or could not be found just before a pet show was about to start. What would they do?

- Encourage students to share related stories about their pets that involve a time when a pet was lost or hurt or afraid of something.

- Create a classroom graph that shows the kinds and numbers of pets your students have.

Some New and Interesting Words from the Story		
told	bragged	entrance
building	favorite	chased
prize	searched	pinned
ribbon	awarded	friends
judges	smiled	independent
join	expect	sorry
talking	start	

Pet Show! *(cont.)*

After Reading the Book

Suggested discussion topics and activities follow:

- Why do you think everyone is so excited about the pet show? Have you ever been to a pet show?

- What kind of fun do you have with others in your neighborhood, school, or community?

- When Archie cannot find the cat, all his friends help him look. Friends often help each other do things, such as find something that is lost, help do a chore or job, or go somewhere together.

- Tell or write about a time when you helped a friend do something special. You may want to use this story starter: Once I helped my friend . . .

- Make sure you tell a lot of details in your story. Answer important questions such as who you helped, what you did to help, when you helped, what happened, and how helping a friend made you feel.

- What does Archie do when he can't find the cat? Does he give up and get mad or just keep looking? How do you think Archie feels when he has to go to the pet show without the cat? What does he do instead? Is this a good idea?

- Tell about a time when you had to decide to do something else because your first choice did not work out. (You may want to discuss the term "alternative" with your students.)

- If you were Archie, how would you feel or what would you have done when the judges gave the old woman the ribbon for the cat? Do you think Archie does the right thing when he tells the woman to keep the ribbon?

- Have you ever done something nice for an older person? Tell what you did and how it made you feel. Can you think of some ways you can be kind or help older citizens in your neighborhood or community? Make a list.

- Archie's mom tells Archie that the cat is independent. What do you think *independent* means? Are some animals more independent than others? In what ways are you independent? Make a list or chart of things that you can do on your own or for yourself.

Sorting Pets

Below are listed many of the pets that are in Archie's neighborhood pet show.
Cut the cards apart and sort them in as many different ways as you can think of.
Add some other animals' names on the blank cards.

Possible ways to sort these pets:

- ❑ by size (little to big)
- ❑ by ABC (alphabetical) order
- ❑ by type of covering (fur, fins, feathers, skin)
- ❑ by type of movement (swims, flies, walks, jumps)
- ❑ by usualness (common or uncommon)

ants	mice	cats
fish	parrots	frogs
canaries	dogs	goldfish
puppies	turtles	germs

Comparative Endings

❑ Use the ER ending (comparative form) to compare two things.
   Example: The dog is bigger than the cat.

❑ Use the EST ending (superlative form) to compare more than two things.
   Example: That dog has the biggest mouth I've ever seen!

❑ Use the root word (positive form) or the ER (comparative form) ending or EST (superlative form) ending from the box below to fill in this chart:

	Positive	Comparative	Superlative
1.		yellower	
2.	busy		busiest
3.		friendlier	friendliest
4.		handsomer	handsomest
5.		noisier	noisiest
6.			brightest
7.		longer	
8.	fast		fastest
9.		softer	
10.	slow		
11.		taller	
12.	quick		

- yellow
- busier
- handsome
- yellowest
- bright
- friendly
- soft
- longest
- noisy
- quicker
- tallest
- faster
- brighter
- slower
- quickest
- tall
- long
- slowest
- softest

You Be the Judge

Name an animal that you think should . . .

❑ win a prize for the longest ears. _____

❑ win a prize for being the slowest. _____

❑ win a prize for being the fastest. _____

❑ win a prize for being the biggest. _____

❑ win a prize for being the smallest. _____

❑ win a prize for being the noisiest. _____

❑ win a prize for being most friendly. _____

❑ win a prize for flying the highest. _____

What animal(s) do you think of when you see these phrases?

❑ ...eats cheese _____ ❑ ...shortest tail _____

❑ ...no tail _____ ❑ ...long whiskers_____

❑ ...softest _____ ❑ ...eats the most_____

❑ ...swims_____ ❑ ...can jump _____

❑ ...lives in a hole_____ ❑ ...lives in a tree _____

❑ ...lives in the water _____ ❑ ...lives alone _____

❑ ...is dangerous _____ ❑ ...is sleek_____

Root Words and Endings

Draw lines to match the root word below with each word from the story:

1. smiled   • ant

2. talking   • judge

3. judges   • pet

4. friends   • long

5. ants   • smile

6. called   • call

7. pets   • talk

8. longest   • friend

9. leaving   • leave

10. walked   • show

11. showed   • pin

12. slowest   • brag

13. bragged   • walk

14. pinned   • search

15. passed   • pass

16. searched   • slow

Pets Together:
Some Silly Sentences

Fill in the blanks with two of the animal names. Then draw a picture for that sentence.

ants	canary	cat	parrot	frog
fish	puppy	dog	turtle	goldfish

❑ The _____ helped the _____ eat pizza one afternoon.

❑ The _____ and the _____ read a book on the beach.

Rhyming Ribbons

On the blank lines write words that rhyme with the words on each ribbon. You may use words from the list to help you.

bold	two	part	send	chart
file	end	hold	gold	you
lend	heart	smile	tile	shoe

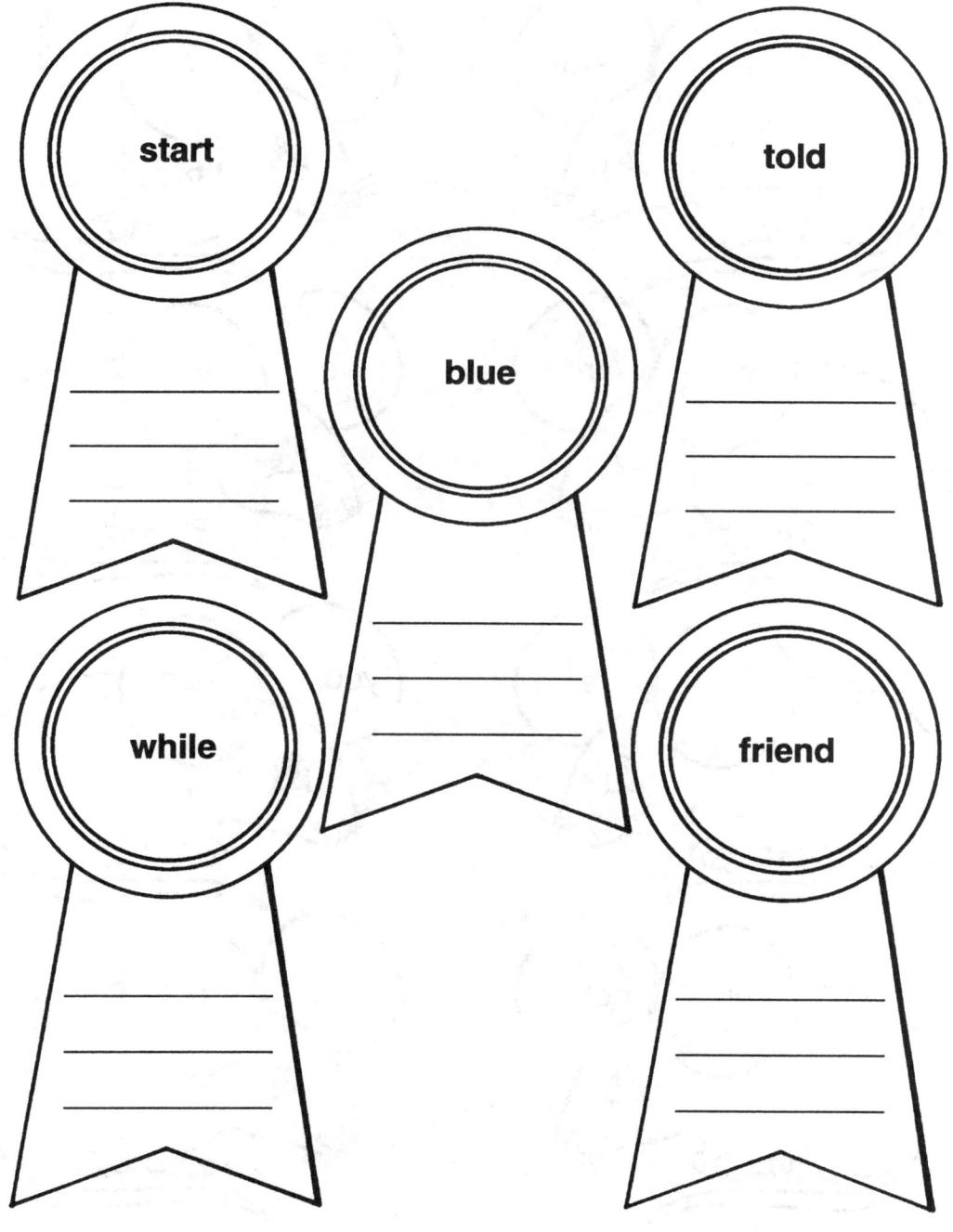

Pet Contractions

Write the contraction for the two words given:

- I'm
- he's
- can't
- you'd
- it's
- you're
- we're
- isn't

Example

1. _____

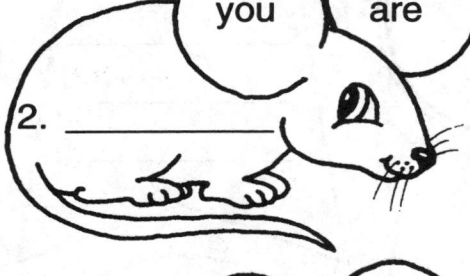

2. _____

3. _____

4. _____

5. _____

6. _____

7. _____

8. _____

Dreams

Summary

One hot night in the city, everyone goes to bed, falls asleep, and begins to dream—except one person. Roberto just cannot fall asleep. Finally he gets up and walks over to the window. To his surprise and dismay, he sees that a big dog has cornered Archie's cat in the box. He is not sure what to do, but he knows he must help. Quite by accident, Roberto knocks over the paper mouse he had made in school. It falls from the window sill and floats down to the street. As it does, the mouse's shadow against the wall gets bigger and bigger and scares away the dog. Finally, Roberto can get to sleep!

Story Map

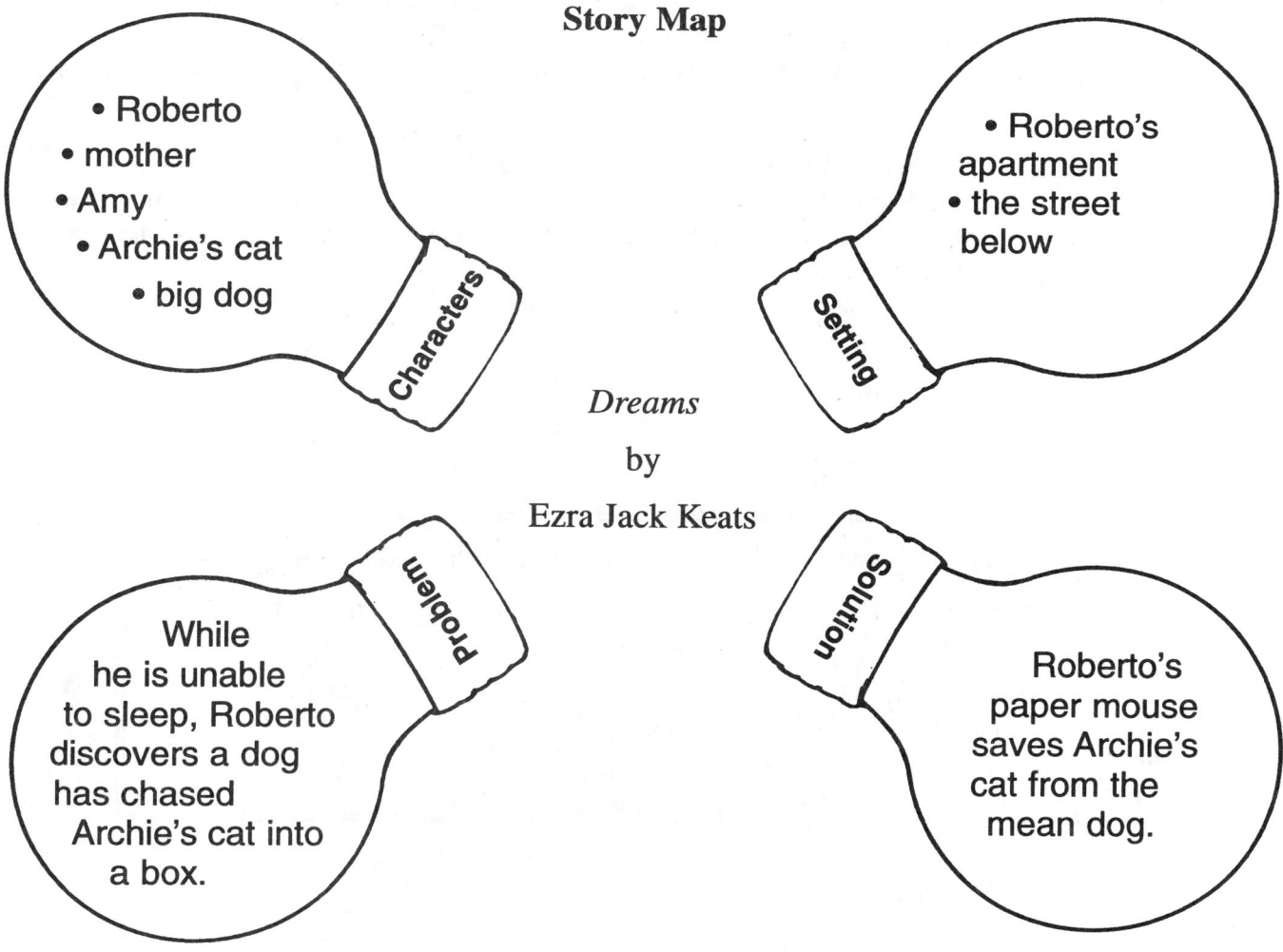

- Roberto
- mother
- Amy
- Archie's cat
- big dog

Characters

- Roberto's apartment
- the street below

Setting

Dreams

by

Ezra Jack Keats

Problem

While he is unable to sleep, Roberto discovers a dog has chased Archie's cat into a box.

Solution

Roberto's paper mouse saves Archie's cat from the mean dog.

Dreams *(cont.)*

Before Reading the Book

Suggested introductory scripts and activities follow:

- Have you ever made a special art project or picture in school? What was it? What did you do with it? What did your friends or family think of it?

- What do you usually do between supper and bedtime? (Get students to suggest after-school activities such as playing with friends, watching TV, doing homework, etc.)

- In the story *Dreams* Roberto is a young boy who lives in the city and can talk to his friends from his apartment window. How might living in a big city be different from living in a small village or town?

- Describe your bedroom. Do you share it with a brother or sister? Do you have a special place for things, such as a shelf or drawer? (See the activity on page 96.)

- What time do you usually go to bed? Do you have a bedtime routine? (Encourage students to list typical things that are done in preparation for bedtime. Have students individually list in order what they do before bedtime. For example, have a snack, change into pajamas, brush teeth, read story, turn off light, etc.

- What is a dream? When do you dream? What is the difference between a dream and a daydream? Have students tell what dreams may be like (funny, scary, sad, happy, mixed up, etc.) Encourage students to tell about dreams they have had or perhaps to describe the nicest dreams they could ever want to have!

- What do you think makes us go to sleep? Why don't we always go to sleep at the same time?

- What is the difference between being sleepy and being tired?

Some New and Interesting Words from the Story

window	dream	trapped
sill	asleep	shadow
darker	street	yawned
quiet	mouse	morning
paper	chased	dashed

Dreams *(cont.)*

After Reading the Book

Suggested discussion topics and activities follow:

- What has Roberto made in school? How do you think Roberto feels when Amy asks him if his mouse can do anything? Why do you think Roberto answers the way he does to Amy?

- Why do you think Roberto cannot sleep?

- Is Roberto having a dream or do you think what he sees really happened?

- In the story, while everyone else goes to sleep, Roberto just cannot fall asleep. Has there ever been a time when you couldn't fall asleep? What did you do? How did you finally get to sleep?

- What are some things that people might do to try to fall asleep? (e.g., listen to music, get a drink of water or warm milk, count sheep, read, etc.)

- Why is getting enough sleep important? What are you like when you are overtired?

- When we go to sleep, many other people are still awake doing jobs, and many things are still going on. Name some people who are still working or things that might be taking place when the rest of us are asleep. (This is an excellent way to introduce a theme on community workers or various careers).

  Some examples might be the following:

  > **Workers:** policemen, firemen, hospital workers, phone operators, garbage collectors, cab drivers, truck drivers, bus drivers, etc.

  > **Events:** mice come out, cats hunt or prowl, babies wake up, bakers make bread, etc.

- Why does the dog run away? What do you think the dog thinks the "shadow" is? What do you think would have happened if the mouse hadn't fallen off the sill?

- Do you think Roberto feels bad about losing his paper mouse? Tell why or why not.

- If the mouse had not fallen, what could Roberto have done to help Archie's cat? What would you have done? What do you think Archie will say the next day when Roberto tells him what happened? Do you think Roberto should tell Amy what the paper mouse did?

Paper Mouse Bookmark Pattern

Directions:

Cut out all pieces. Paste the head onto the body as shown. Then paste ears on the head. Paste one end of the tail under the body and write a personal message on the tail. Add string or yarn for whiskers.

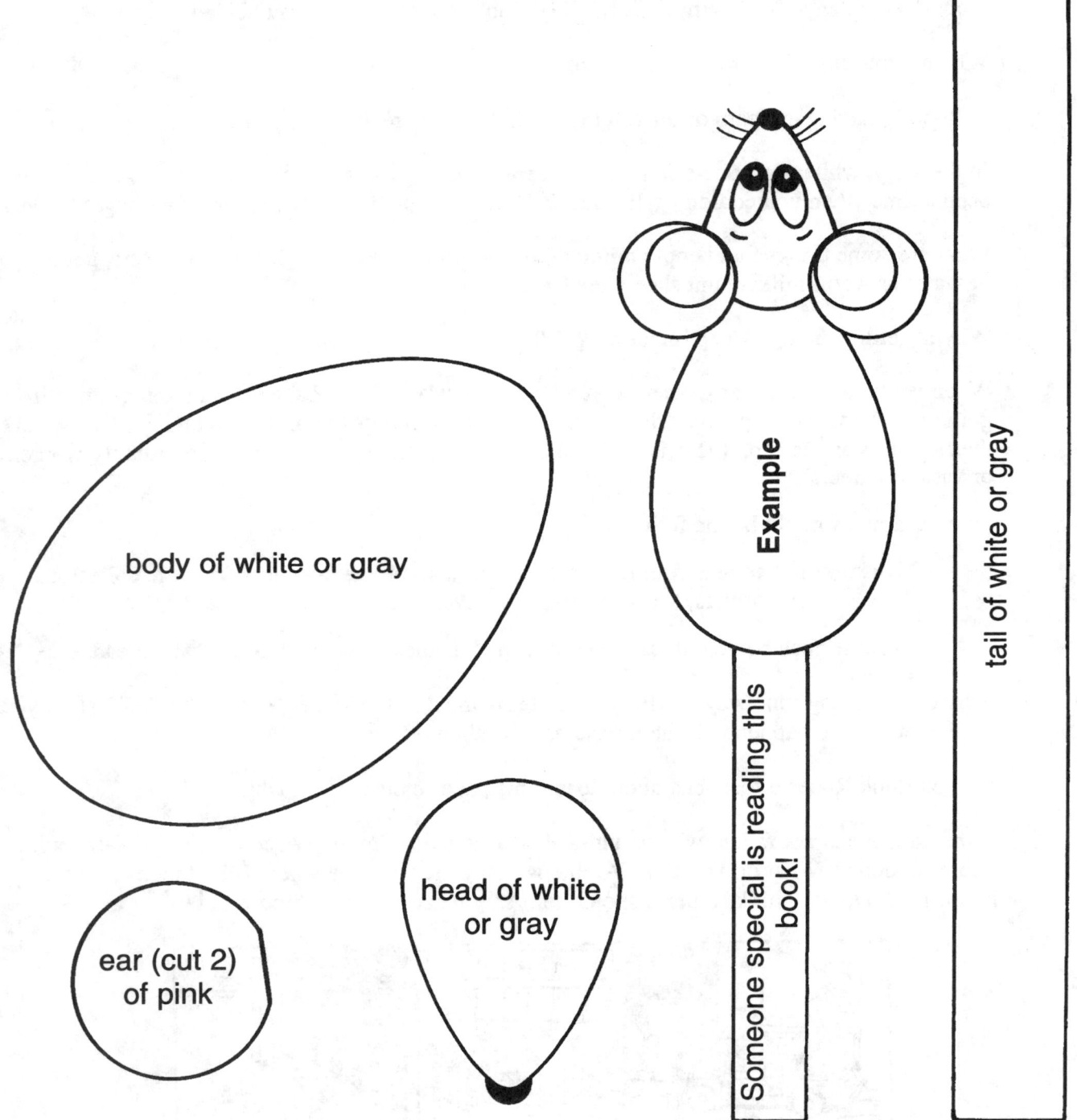

Example

body of white or gray

Someone special is reading this book!

tail of white or gray

ear (cut 2) of pink

head of white or gray

Rhyming Pairs

If the word pairs below rhyme, color the happy face. If they do not rhyme, color the sad face.

1. mouse   house   ☺   ☹

2. sill   hill   ☺   ☹

3. dream   sleeve   ☺   ☹

4. wait   late   ☺   ☹

5. part   dark   ☺   ☹

6. big   bit   ☺   ☹

7. hot   dot   ☺   ☹

8. snarl   howl   ☺   ☹

9. street   heat   ☺   ☹

10. box   socks   ☺   ☹

My Bedroom

Draw a picture of your bedroom.

[drawing box]

❑ Is your bedroom on the 1st, 2nd, or 3rd floor? _____

❑ Do you share a bedroom? With whom?_____

❑ What color is your bedroom? _____

❑ Do you have a special place for books, toys, or other things? Where is it?

_____

❑ What is the very best thing about your bedroom? _____

_____

_____

Matching Characters and Actions

Draw a line to match the right character from the story with the action or event that is related to that character.

1. She asked Roberto if his mouse did anything.

   • the dog

2. She told Roberto that it was his bedtime.

   • Roberto

3. It echoed the words, "G-o-o-o-d Night!"

   • the mouse's shadow

4. He couldn't fall asleep.

   • Amy

5. It was trapped in a box.

   • the paper mouse

6. It chased a cat.

   • the parrot

7. It fell off the window sill.

   • Mother

8. It got bigger and bigger.

   • Archie's cat

Sequencing

Number the events on each mouse in the order they happened.

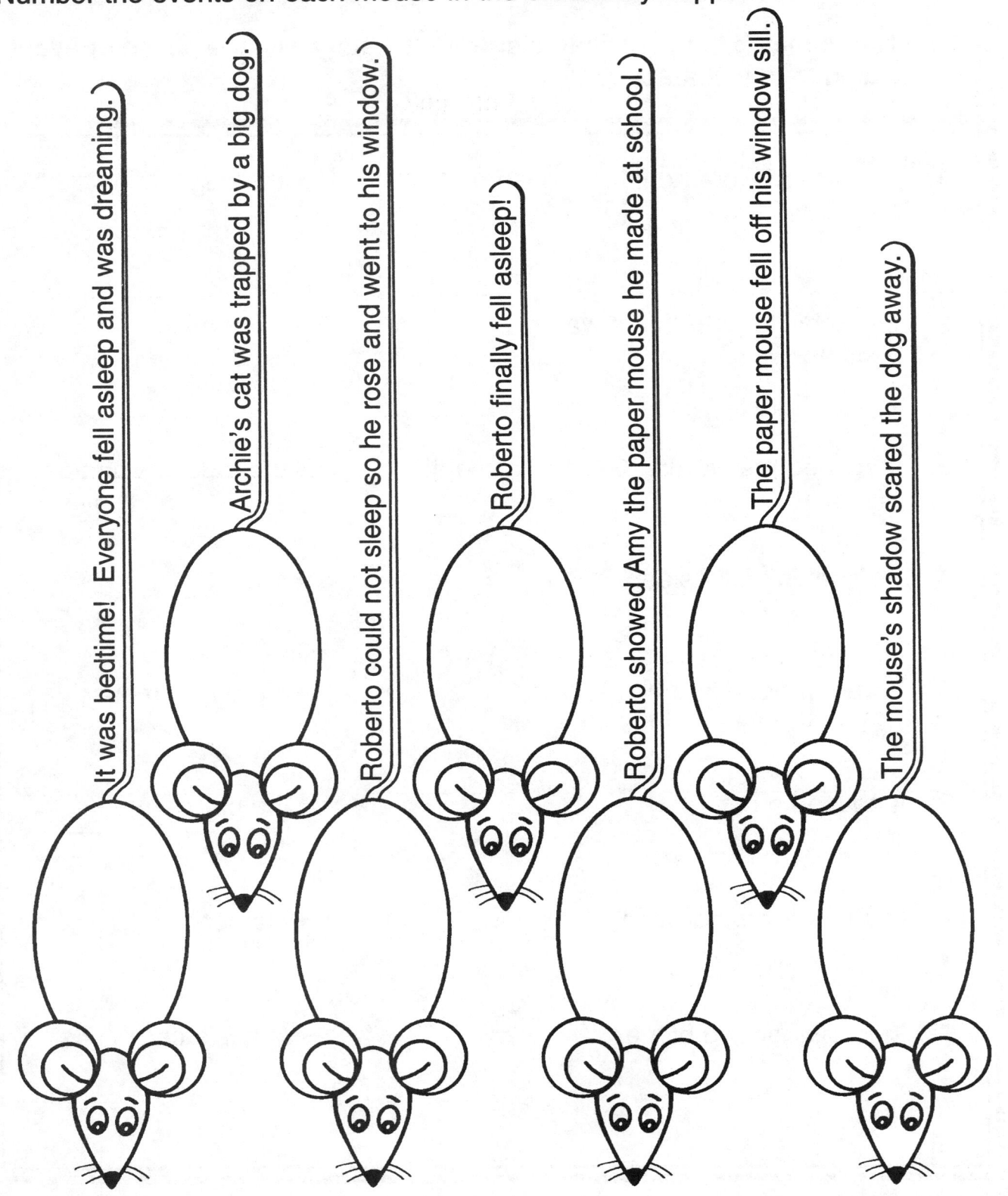

It was bedtime! Everyone fell asleep and was dreaming.

Archie's cat was trapped by a big dog.

Roberto could not sleep so he rose and went to his window.

Roberto finally fell asleep!

Roberto showed Amy the paper mouse he made at school.

The paper mouse fell off his window sill.

The mouse's shadow scared the dog away.

What Was It About?

Sometimes when we sleep, we dream. Dreams can be happy, sad, funny, mixed up, scary, real, or magical.

❑ Did you ever have a happy or funny dream? _____

What was it about? _____

_____

_____

_____

_____

_____

_____

❑ Did you ever have a sad or scary dream? _____

Tell what that dream was about. _____

_____

_____

_____

_____

_____

_____

_____

Opposite Ears

Cut out the ears on the next page and paste them on the mice in pairs of opposite words.

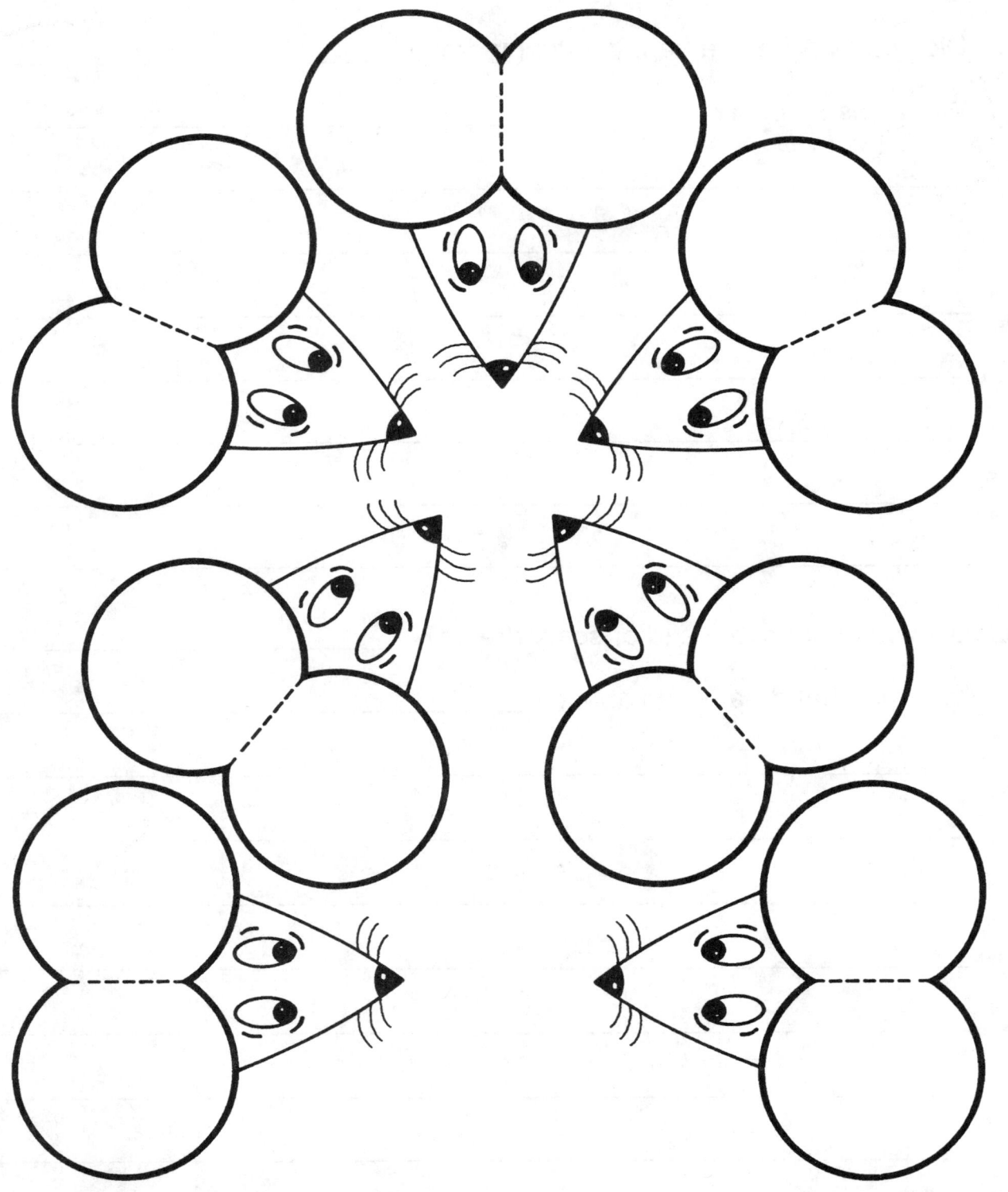

Opposite Ears *(cont.)*

Cut out the ears and arrange them in opposite pairs on the mice on the page before this.

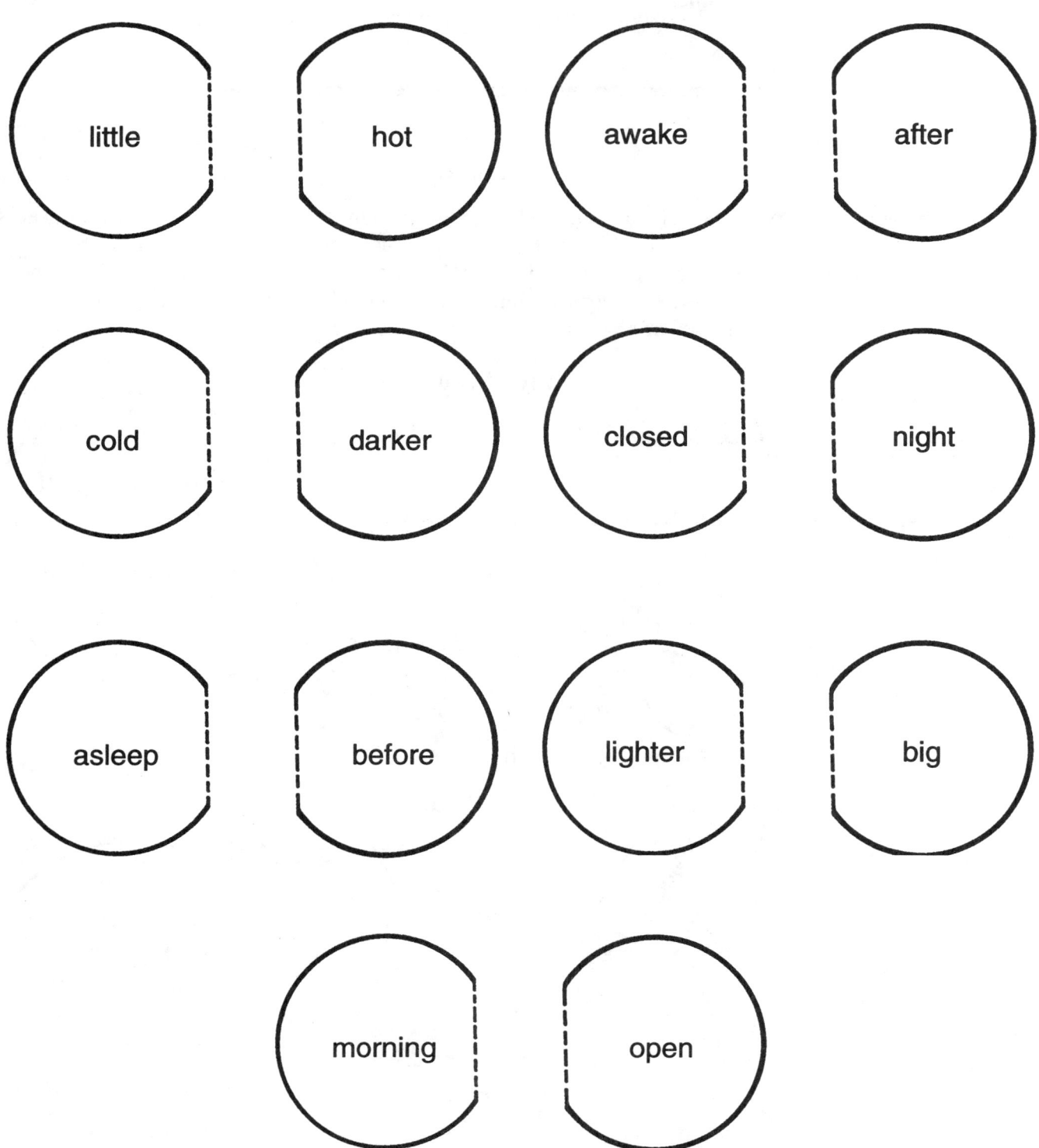

Maggie and the Pirate

Themes

- Friendship
- Families
- Pets
- Nontraditional Homes

Summary

Maggie and her family live on an island. While Maggie is out running some errands, her pet cricket is stolen by someone identifying himself as a pirate. Along with her good friends, Paco and Katie, Maggie sets out to find the pirate and get her pet back. They discover the "pirate" is a new boy who is lonely in many ways. After a scuffle to retrieve Maggie's stolen cricket, the children learn some valuable information about the loss of a pet and the discovery of a new friend.

Story Map

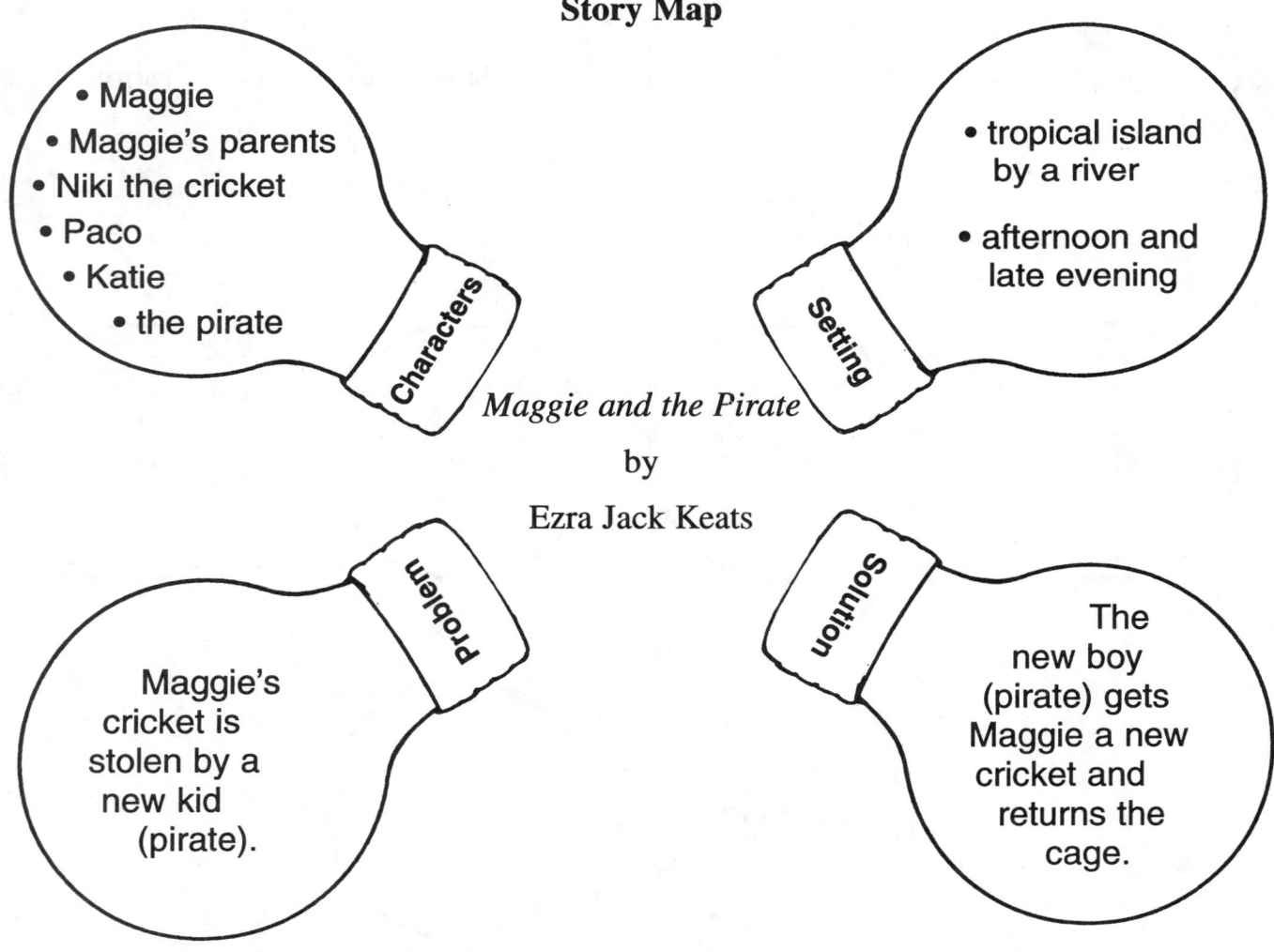

Characters
- Maggie
- Maggie's parents
- Niki the cricket
- Paco
- Katie
- the pirate

Setting
- tropical island by a river
- afternoon and late evening

Maggie and the Pirate

by

Ezra Jack Keats

Problem

Maggie's cricket is stolen by a new kid (pirate).

Solution

The new boy (pirate) gets Maggie a new cricket and returns the cage.

Maggie and the Pirate *(cont.)*

Before Reading the Book

Suggested introductory scripts and activities follow:

- Introduce the setting of the story by using the word *tropical* and describing what is typically thought of as representative of tropical. Compare the area where the students presently live (type and size of community and geographic features) to that of a tropical island.

- Describe styles of dress and fashion that are considered tropical. Draw tropical patterns or murals.

- Discuss the various types of pets that students might have. Does anyone have an unusual pet? Are certain types of pets more or less important or lovable because of the kinds of animals they are? What makes any animal a "pet"? Discuss what types of pets a child living on a tropical island might have.

- Write the word *pirate* on the board. Have students take turns telling what they think of when they hear this word. If age-appropriate, ask students to look up the word *pirate* in a dictionary to compare meanings. Ask students to draw pictures of pirates or describe what a pirate could look like.

- Have students make a chart to compare how they live to how they might live if they were on a tropical island. Fold a paper in half and use each side to write ideas or information. For example, on the "Where I Live Now" side, they may write that they go to the mall to shop and to the park to play. On the "Tropical Island" half of the paper, they may suggest that they would not have big malls to go to, and they would play in the jungle or on a beach instead of in a park.

Some New and Interesting Words from the Story

pirate	grocery	straggled
cage	paddles	starve
cricket	appeared	strength
horror	beautiful	familiar
hideout	joined	buried
scuffled	chirping	

Maggie and the Pirate *(cont.)*

After Reading the Book

Suggested discussion topics and activities follow:

- Where does Maggie live? How do you think her family fixed up the inside of the old bus?

- Name different kinds of houses and places where people can live. (e.g., houses, mobile homes, houseboats, RV's, tents, apartments, cabins, etc.)

- Discussing nontraditional homes may lead to a discussion about homeless people and what really constitutes a "home." (This type of values discussion should be conducted in a sensitive manner, especially considering the possible various homes or home situations of your students.)

- Is Maggie happy living there with her family? Why do you think so? (Have students look through the story to find evidence to support their opinions about this.) Some examples which can be used to suggest Maggie is happy are found in passages relating to the following:

  —Maggie is willing to do things to help her mother.

  —She is outside playing contentedly.

  —Maggie's pop builds her a new cage for her pet.

  —Maggie has friends around her and spends time with them.

  —Maggie's friends call her "lucky."

- What is your favorite part of the story?

- What is the reason the pirate gives for stealing Maggie's cricket? Does that reason make it all right for him to take it? Is it ever all right to take something that does not belong to you?

- Maggie lives by a river and uses a homemade raft to cross it and to get places. What are some other ways (means of transportation) people use to get around? Have students design a picture or posters showing various means of transportation. Ask students to brainstorm for a list of ways we get around. Group the kinds of transportation given into three categories: Land, Air, and Water. Take a poll to see how many students have ever used the various means of transportation. Graph your results.

Sequencing Strips

Each sentence strip tells an event that happened in the book. Cut the 10 strips apart and arrange them in the correct order according to the story. Paste them on a blank sheet of paper.

Note to Teachers: For variation, use fewer strips for younger students or reproduce sentences on large, cardboard strips and do this as a class activity. Also, older students can copy the sentences in the correct order on another paper.

Maggie hung Niki's cage on a tree.

Niki and the cage were gone!

The pirate gave Maggie a new cricket.

Maggie went to look for the pirate.

Maggie was feeding her pet cricket, Niki.

She found a tree house she hadn't seen before.

Maggie fought with the pirate!

The tree house fell into the water.

On her way to get groceries for her mom, Maggie picked up her friends, Paco and Katie.

Niki drowned. They buried Niki.

Finding Friends

Fill in the spaces in the first column about yourself. Then, following your teacher's directions, walk around the room and find another person who shares the same answer as you do. Have that person sign his or her name in the space in the second column. Find as many different friends as you can to sign your sheet.

Facts	You	Friends with the Same Answer
1. favorite color		
2. favorite animal or pet		
3. number of pets		
4. month of your birthday		
5. color of eyes		
6. favorite food		
7. color of house or trailer where you live		
8. a sport or game you enjoy		
9. favorite school subject		
10. number of letters in your first name		

Homes

Maggie's cricket lived in a cage, but in nature many creatures have their own special places to live. Write the names of the living beings near their pictures. Then draw a line to match each to its home.

cave

tree

house

under a rock

lake

underground hole

ocean

Invent a Pet

Maggie's pet cricket is an unusual but real pet.

❑ Think of some other animals that we think of as pets:

_____ _____

_____ _____

_____ _____

❑ Can you think of a real animal that makes an unusual pet?

_____ _____

❑ Invent a new pet by taking parts of one kind of animal and putting them together with parts of another animal.

Example: An elephant with a very tall neck like that of a giraffe might be called an ELEGIRAFFE or maybe a GIRAPHANT.

Think of two (or more) animals that you could use to make an imaginary new pet. Which animals will you use?

_____ _____

❑ What will your new "pet" be called?

_____

❑ Where will you keep it?

_____

❑ What will it eat?

_____

❑ Below, on the back of this paper, or on another piece of paper, draw a picture of your new pet!

The Shopping List

Maggie's mother gave her a grocery list to use for shopping.

But her grocery list got mixed up with two other lists. Sort the items below and write then on the correct list at the bottom of the page.

potatoes	wrench	apples	cake
wire	shoes	hammer	hat
soda	socks	skirt	oatmeal
boots	rake	nails	sweatshirt
milk	pipe	pants	pie
gloves	meat	shovel	bolts

Food	Clothes	Tools

Bibliography

Anderson, Brian. *Ezra Jack Keats: Artist and Picture Book Maker.* World Publishers, 1985.

Engel, Dean and Florence B. Freedman. *Ezra Jack Keats: A Biography for Young Readers.* Silver Moon, 1994.

Freedman, Florence B. *"Ezra Jack Keats: Author and Illustrator," Elementary English,* Hunter College, City University of New York.

More Jr. Authors, "Ezra Jack Keats," page 120.

Phi Delta Kappan, "Ezra Jack Keats. . . the consummate artist. . . the careful writer."

Something About the Author, "Keats, Ezra Jack," Volume 4, 1984.

Stewig, John Warren. *Reading Pictures, Exploring Illustrations with Children: Ezra Jack Keats.* Jenson Publishing Inc., Wisconsin, 1988.

Young and Old, Macmillan Literature-Based Reading Activities, "Meet the Author: Ezra Jack Keats." Newbridge Communication, Inc., 1991.

Other Books by Ezra Jack Keats

Kitten for a Day. Macmillan, 1993.
(Available in Canada and AUS from Macmillan; in UK from Maxwell Macmillan)

Little Drummer Boy. Macmillan, 1987.
(Available in Canada and AUS from Macmillan; in UK from Maxwell Macmillan)

Louie. Greenwillow, 1983.
(Available in Canada from Gage Distributors; in UK from International Book Distributors; in AUS from Kirby Book Company)

Regards to the Man on the Moon. Macmillan, 1987.
(Available in Canada from Gage Distributors; in UK from International Book Distributors; in AUS from Kirby Book Company)

Snowy Day. Scholastic, 1993.

The Trip. William Morrow, 1987.
(Available in Canada from Gage Distributors; in UK from International Book Distributors; in AUS from Kirby Book Company)

Answer Key

Page 20

1. couldn't
2. I'll
3. Wouldn't
4. he's
5. I've
6. It's

Page 22

when/ever, no/thing, side/walk, him/self, every/thing, out/side

Page 25

3 1 2
1 3 2
2 3 4 1

Page 29

Jennie waits for her hat to come.
She opens the box she got from her aunt.
She thinks her hat is too plain.
Jennie tries on other things to use for a hat.
Jennie feeds the birds on Saturday afternoon.
She goes to church with her family.
The birds decorate her hat for her.
Jennie and her mother wrap her wonderful hat.

Page 30

fancy—plain
beautiful—ugly
appeared—disappeared
shutting—opening
opened—closed
shiny—dull
same—different
early—late
proud—ashamed
aunt—uncle
add—subtract
real—fake
big—little
mother—father
started—stopped
filled—emptied
quiet—loud
after—before

Page 31

The following 15 squares should be colored orange to form a path from top to bottom:

leaves, a big orange leaf, violet flowers, a big red rose, paper fan, a pink Valentine, a big green leaf, a nest of chirping birds, colored eggs, more real flowers, picture of swans on a lake, paper flowers, a big yellow rose, more pictures, colored paper

Page 34

1. d
2. t
3. ed
4. d
5. d
6. t
7. t
8. t
9. ed
10. t
11. ed
12. d
13. d
14. t
15. t

Page 38

d, g, a, f, c, h, e, b.

Page 39

bone—Willie
toy crocodile—Peter
rattle—Susie
crib—Susie
bowl—Willie
cookies—Peter
high chair—Susie
collar—Willie
blue chair—Peter
blocks—Peter
bootie—Susie
sneakers—Peter

Page 40

didn't
we'll
it's
couldn't
that's
won't
you'll
wasn't

Page 42

start—finish
high—low
quietly—loudly
baby—adult
sister—brother
leave—stay
tall—short
do—don't
whispered—yelled
stood—sat
full—empty
happy—sad
ceiling—floor

mother-father
outside-inside
front-back

Page 47

1. Mail: stamp, envelope, letter
2. Weather: wind, rain, thunder
3. Animals: dog, parrot, cat
4. Birthdays: party, cake, candle

Page 50

1. raincoat
2. wind
3. water
4. lightning
5. foggy
6. clouds

Page 51

The following parrots should be colored:
1, 3, 4, 6, 7

Page 58

Compound Word Match: hideout, everyone, something, motorcycle, footsteps

Page 59

1. happy
2. mean
3. brave
4. scared
5. proud

Page 66

1. dog—cat
2. Archie—Peter
3. croaked—giggled
4. big—tall
5. ice cream—cake
6. Grandpa—Grandma
7. hand—ear
8. black—brown
9. book—bag
10. hat—sweater

Page 67

suddenly—sudden
croaked—croak
tallest—tall
harder—hard
laughing—laugh
closer—close
children—child
waiting—wait
shaky—shake
obeyed—obey

Page 69

verbs:
1. purred, walked

Answer Key

2. wagged
3. meowed
4. nuzzled
5. jumped
6. perked, heard
7. ran
8. raced
9. barked
10. growled

6 animal names: cat, dog, horse, kitty, puppy, gerbil

root words: wag, meow, perk, nuzzle, jump, race

Page 70
Showing Respect: HAVE RESPECT

Page 71
block, corner, looked, mustache, obeyed, paper, store, tallest, voice, world

Page 75
Word Search:

ABC Order:

1. apartment
2. blind
3. building
4. city
5. colors
6. family
7. harmonica
8. lonely
9. music
10. played
11. rain
12. sights
13. smells
14. sounds

Page 78
City: movie houses, tall apartment buildings, many stores/factories, subways, restaurants, busy streets.

Country: cows in a pasture, fields of corn, big open gardens, tractors plowing, horses in a field, barns/silos.

Pages 79–80

Apartment	Strip
1	A
2	E
3	L
4	I
5	B
6	H
7	G
8	D
9	K
10	F
11	C
12	J

Page 85

ROOT	ER	EST
yellow	yellower	yellowest
busy	busier	busiest
friendly	friendlier	friendliest
handsome	handsomer	handsomest
noisy	noisier	noisiest
bright	brighter	brightest
long	longer	longest
fast	faster	fastest
soft	softer	softest
slow	slower	slowest
tall	taller	tallest
quick	quicker	quickest

Page 87
smiled—smile
talking—talk
judges—judge
friends—friend
ants—ant
called—call
pets—pet
longest—long
leaving—leave
walked—walk
showed—show
slowest—slow
bragged—brag
pinned—pin
passed—pass
searched—search

Page 89
1. start—heart, part, chart
2. told—bold, hold, gold
3. blue —two, you, shoe
4. while—file, smile, tile
5. friend—lend, end, send

Page 90
1. I'm
2. you're
3. it's
4. can't
5. he's
6. we're
7. you'd
8. isn't

Page 95
1. yes
2. yes
3. no
4. yes
5. no
6. no
7. yes
8. no
9. yes
10. yes

Page 97
1. Amy
2. Mother
3. the parrot
4. Roberto
5. Archie's cat
6. the dog
7. the paper mouse
8. the mouse's shadow.

Page 98
1. Roberto showed Amy the paper mouse.
2. It was bedtime! Everyone...
3. Roberto could not sleep so he...
4. Archie's cat was trapped by a...
5. The paper mouse fell off his...
6. The mouse's shadow scared the dog
7. Roberto finally fell asleep!

Pages 100–101
hot—cold, after—before, darker—lighter, night—morning, asleep—awake, big—little, open—closed

Page 105
1 – Maggie was feeding her pet cricket, Niki.
2 – Maggie hung Niki's cage on a tree.
3 – On her way to get groceries for her mom, Maggie picked up her friends, Paco and Katie.
4 – Niki and the cage were gone!
5 – Maggie went to look for the pirate.
6 – She found a tree house she hadn't seen before.
7 – Maggie fought with the pirate!
8 – The tree house fell into the water.
9 – Niki drowned. They buried Niki.
10 – The pirate gave Maggie a new cricket.

Page 107
bird—tree
snake—(worm)-under rock
bat—cave
swan(duck)—lake
person—house
whale(fish)—ocean
gopher—underground hole

Page 109

Food	Clothes	Tools
potatoes	boots	wire
soda	gloves	wrench
milk	shoes	rake
meat	socks	pipe
apples	skirt	hammer
cake	pants	nails
oatmeal	hat	shovel
pie	sweatshirt	bolts